Under Construction

by
Rhonda Paisley

AMBASSADOR

Kids Under Construction
© Copyright 1993 Rhonda Paisley

ISBN 907927 95 5

All rights reserved

Ambassador Productions Ltd,
16 Hillview Avenue,
Belfast, BT5 6JR
Northern Ireland, UK

Author's Note

This daily reading book has been designed to help children form the habit of including God in their daily life.

It is not a child's Bible, nor is it an exhaustive theological discourse! Rather, it is a tool to help children develop the simple principle of knowing their God by building a personal relationship with Him day by day. Church going, Sunday School attendance, memorising Scripture have their place - but these things can so easily become empty ritual and vain repetition if they have not their foundation based upon a personal friendship with the King of kings!

It is my sincere desire that Kids Under Construction will be of much help to the child who uses it and that the enjoyment to be found by honouring the Word of God will be theirs not just through the days of their childhood but throughout life.

Rhonda Paisley
Belfast,
September, 1993

*Dedicated with love to
Lydia, Kara and Shane my neices and nephew
and to Matthew, my little friend*

My sincere thanks are due to:-

My sister, Cherith, who transformed my handwritten script into clear type and created the layout in preparation for printing. Her advice and guidance with this task along with her time and patience have been invaluable to me.

My mother, who had the unenviable task of proof reading the script and who along with my Father encouraged me to transform my initial idea for the book into a reality.

Mr. Joe Costley and Mr. Sam Lowry who, when approached with the idea were enthusiastic and practical with their advice and help.

About the Author

Rhonda Paisley is the second of five children born to Ian and Eileen Paisley. She is by profession an artist. She studied fine art at BJU, Greenville, South Carolina, USA, graduating in 1981 with a BA in fine art and minor in English. She also took a certificate course in Victorian art and literature at London University and holds a T.E.F.L. certificate. Her paintings have been shown in solo exhibitions in the United States, Belfast and Dublin.

In 1988 Rhonda wrote the book, 'Ian Paisley, My Father' which was published in both hardback and paperback.

For five years Rhonda worked among Belfast's unemployed young people and drug addicts. During this time she ran a drop in centre in Belfast where she held a seat on the City Council for eight years.

Currently Rhonda is involved in exhibition work and writes a weekly column for Northern Ireland's largest morning newspaper.

Bibliography

Christian Foundations; Paisley, Ian R. K.
Martyrs Memorial Productions, Belfast
3rd Edition, 1984.

Bible Cyclopaedia; Eadie, John.
Religious Tract Sos,
London 1881.

Numbers in Scripture; Bullinger, E. W.
Eyre & Spottiswoode, London
3rd Edition, 1913.

Analytical Concordance to the Holy Bible; Young, Robert.
Lutterworth Press, London
8th Edition, 1953.

What About Heaven; Scroggie, W. Graham.
Pickering & Ingles Ltd.,
London, 1954.

Christian Behaviour; Lewis, C.S.
Centenary Press,
London, 1943.

List of Contents

JANUARY
  ❖ Creation 9
FEBRUARY
  ❖ Heaven 25
MARCH
  ❖ Prayer 41
APRIL
  ❖ Numbers and Colours 57
MAY
  ❖ Miracles 73
JUNE
  ❖ Plants & Animals 89
JULY
  ❖ Heroes 105
AUGUST
  ❖ Parables 121
SEPTEMBER
  ❖ The Ten Commandments 137
OCTOBER
  ❖ Contentment 153
NOVEMBER
  ❖ Gifts 169
DECEMBER
  ❖ Jesus 185

9 JANUARY

It took God six busy days of work to make the earth, the sky and the seas and then to fill them with birds, fish and animals. His most special creation was man and woman because they were made in His image. That means they were made like Him. You can understand this if you get a mirror and look in it. The person you see is just like you - but it isn't really you. It is just what we call a reflection, or an image of you. The person you see in the mirror cannot do anything by itself - you have to make that person wink or smile or stick out its tongue! (Try this and see!)

God has made us like Him but we cannot do all the things which God can do, just as your reflection by itself cannot do all the things which you can do.

Why don't you draw a picture of your reflection.

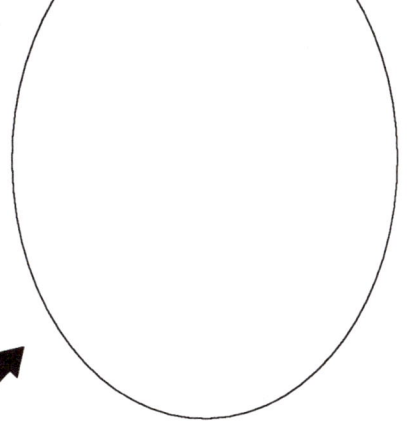

10 JANUARY

The very first man that God made was called Adam. God called him Adam because the word Adam means 'the man'.

Do you know what your name means?

In order to make Adam, God took dust from the earth, and made it into a man.

You and I could never do this but we can make many other things with our hands. We can make shapes out of plasticine, playdough and clay.

Then, when God had made the dust into the shape of Adam He breathed into Adam the breath of life and so Adam became alive.

If you have some plasticine you could make a shape out of it. You could make an animal or a man or may be a bird. But you won't be able to make it come alive!

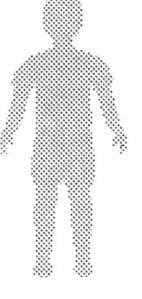

11 JANUARY

You and I have a home to live in. Adam had a very special home which God made for him. It wasn't a building. It was a garden which God Himself planted. This garden was set Eastward in Eden. There are four main directions on earth. They are North, South, East and West.

In this special garden God grew every tree that not only was lovely to look at, but that provided good food.

He also placed in the middle of the garden a unique tree - the tree of knowledge of good and evil.

Can you remember what direction the garden faced?

How many main directions are there on earth?

12 JANUARY

Trees and plants need water in order to grow. So through the garden which was made for Adam God put a river. This river divided into four rivers after it ran through the garden. These rivers all provided water for other parts of the earth outside the garden. Their names are very unusual so do not worry if you cannot remember them. They are **PISON, GIHON, HIDDEKEL** and **EUPHRATES**.

It is more important to remember to keep our rivers nice and clean so that the plants which God made will have good water to help them grow.

How many rivers did the garden river divide into?

13 JANUARY

When God put Adam into this lovely garden for his home He told him that he was to look after the garden and keep it tidy. God also made a rule that Adam had to keep. This special instruction was the he must not eat the food of the unique tree - the tree of the knowledge of good and evil. Adam was allowed to eat from every other tree except this one. God told Adam that if he ate from this tree he would 'surely die'. So you can see how important it was that Adam obeyed God.

Can you think of an important rule that you must keep? For example you must not run across the road.

14 JANUARY

God did not just make a man. He also made a woman.
The very first woman was made by God so that Adam could have a friend to help him. To make this woman God made Adam go to sleep and while he was sleeping God took one of Adam's ribs and out of that rib he created a woman.
Adam did not feel any pain while God was doing this because he was in a very very deep sleep. Adam called his wife's name Eve. Adam also gave names to all the animals and birds which God had created.

Do you have names for your toys? Why don't you draw one of your toys and write its name beside it.

15 JANUARY

Let's see how much we can remember about creation
You fill in the gaps.

★ On the **FIRST** day of creation God said:
 '_ _ _   _ _ _ _ _ _   _ _   _ _ _ _ _ _ :   _ _ _   _ _ _
 _ _   _ _ _   _ _ _ _ _'

★ On the **SECOND** day of creation God made Heaven. Can you remember the big word to describe this?
 F_ _ _ _ _ _ _ _

★ The **THIRD** thing which God made was the **E** _ **RT** _.

★ On the **FOURTH** day He made special lights - one for the day time and one for the night time. We call these the **S** _ _ and the **M** _ _ _. He also made the **S** _ _ _ _ _.

★ On the **FIFTH** day God made **F** _ _ _ and **B** _ _ **D** _.

★ The same day as God made animals He made man and woman. This was the **S** _ _ _ _ day of creation.

16 JANUARY

Do you enjoy Sunday?

What do you do to show your love for God on Sunday?

It took God six busy days of work to create our beautiful world. When God had finished making all these things He looked at them and saw that they were well made. God's work of creation was finished so, on the seventh day He rested and didn't do any work at all. We also need to rest each week, don't we? Imagine how hard it would be to have to go to school on Saturday and Sunday as well as all the other days of the week!
God created a rest day for us to enjoy. We use that day to love Him, worship him and to admire His creation.

1 JANUARY

Do you know what the word 'created' means? It means God made a beautiful world for us to live in and to enjoy. If you look all around, you can see just how amazing are the things God created. Invisible fresh air for us to breathe. Bright colours painted onto flowers. Furry animals to have for pets and big wild animals to keep the forests and jungles tidy. He made huge seas for us to sail and filled them with all sorts of fish. He even put slippery jelly fish into them and crabs that nip, and strange plants that grow under water. Over all of this He hung a big sky and each day He puts different things into it - clouds, stars, rain, wind, the sun and the moon.
This is our world. God made it for us.

Can you draw a picture of what you saw in the world today?

2 JANUARY

Do you know what the every first thing was that God created?
The first thing He created was light.
In the first book of the Bible, which is called Genesis, it tells us that God said:-
'Let there be light: and there was light'
It was very important that God made light first. It meant that He could divide day from night. So, the first day was made and it had a morning and an evening because there was light and there was darkness. Each day we enjoy the light which God created and each night we can sleep in the darkness so that we are rested and healthy.

Can you find which verse in Genesis chapter one where God said, 'Let there be light: and there was light'?

3 JANUARY

The second thing which God made has a very big name. It is called the firmament. Although this is a big word to say it is an easy word to understand, because God called the firmament 'Heaven'. By the time God had finished making heaven it was evening time so the second day of creation was over.

Why don't you see if you can remember how to spell the very big name that means Heaven.

F _ _ _ _ _ _ _ _

4 JANUARY

On the third day of creation God made dry land appear. This is what we call the earth. Around the dry land he placed lots of water. These waters are what we call seas. We have many different seas.

The earth which God created is divided into different continents and the continents are divided into countries.

God formed the earth so that it was able to have trees and grass, plants and flowers, fruit and vegetables all grow on it.

All these things make the earth very pleasant and beautiful for us.

Do you know in what continent your country is?

Do you know what sea is nearest to where you live?

Do you know the name of the country in which you live?

5 JANUARY

Do you ever wonder where the sun comes from? Do you ever wonder why there is a moon in the sky and hundreds of stars around it? Well, God made the sun and set it in the sky so that the earth, the seas, the animals, the plants and you and I would have heat. We need the warmth of the sun so that things will grow and so that we won't be too cold. If we were too cold we would not be able to live! The sun is a greater light than the moon.

The moon is very important as well. If we had no moon in the darkness of the night we would not be able to see very much! The stars also provide beauty and light. God must like the stars very much because He made a special star for His Son, Jesus Christ.

God made the sun, the moon and the stars during the fourth day of His work.

Can you draw the sun, the moon and the stars?

Don't forget which is the biggest!

6 JANUARY

The day after God made the sun, moon and stars he made some other things which we can see in the sky. Can you guess what they are? They have wings and can fly. There are small ones and large ones. They have feathers. Some of their feathers are very bright and colourful, some are simply black and brown. You know what they are, don't you? They are the birds of the air and they sing lovely songs of thanks to God for creating them.

Not only did God make the birds on the fifth day of His work, but He also made lots and lots of different fish to swim in the seas. He made massive whales and sleek dolphins. He made sharks with sharp spiky teeth. He made smaller fish as well and some of these He made as brightly coloured as the feathers of the birds.

Do you have a favourite bird? Maybe you have a pet goldfish. Can you name a type of bird and a type of fish?

7 JANUARY

When God had put lots of fish into the sea and when He had made plenty of birds to fly in the sky He decided to make animals to live in the earth.
He made a great assortment of animals and creatures - tall ones like elephants, small ones like mice. Fat ones like pigs and thin ones like snakes. He made furry ones and baldy ones! He made strong ones and weak ones. He made fast panthers and cheetahs. He made slow tortoises. He made proud lions and shy reindeers. He made animals and creatures that like the night and ones that would rather have the day.
God designed all these animals and creatures to live in the earth. He gave some of them very beautiful skins and coats. He made some of them with stripes and spots, and he made some of them plain and simply coloured.

 Why don't you draw a picture of your favourite animal.

8 JANUARY

On the sixth day of God's work when He had finished making the animals, God decided to make man and woman. He gave man and woman a very special job to do. Do you know what that job was?
It was to rule over the animals and creatures, the fish and the birds.

List three things that you do to help look after the earth.

God told them to 'subdue the earth'. That means it was their job to keep the earth under good control - to look after it and all the things God had made for it. This is why we must be careful not to throw rubbish all over the ground. It is why we must be kind and loving to the animals which God made. It is why we must keep the seas clean for the fish to live in and it is why we need to feed the birds in winter when it is too cold for them to find their own food.
God has given us this very special job and it is important to obey the very first thing He asked man and woman to do.

25 JANUARY

Here are some questions for you to answer. See how many you can get right!

- ★ Did God make a special day for us to rest on? Yes ☐ No ☐
- ★ Can you give two words beginning with the letter 'G' which tell us about God?
  G _ _ _ _ and G _ _ _ .
- ★ The S _ _ P _ _ T told Eve a lie.
- ★ Did Eve listen to the serpent? Yes ☐ No ☐
- ★ Who did Eve give some of the food to?
  A _ _ _ .
- ★ Adam and Eve felt what when they disobeyed the rule?
  S _ _ M _ .
- ★ Did Adam and Eve hide? Yes ☐ No ☐
- ★ Before God put Adam and Eve out of the garden what did He make them?
  C _ _ _ _ of _ K _ N _ .
- ★ What things did God place at the east of the garden to protect the way to the tree of life?
  C _ _ _ U _ _ _ _ and a F _ _ _ _ N _ S _ _ _ _ .

26 JANUARY

Let's think about our mirror again. Remember the big black ✗ we talked about? Well in a way when Adam and Eve disobeyed God they put a big black ✗ between them and their friendship with God. Because God loved Adam and Eve and all their children, He decided that He would remove the mark that distorted their friendship. In order to do this God had to make a special plan. This plan involved His very own Son who is called Jesus. If you really did paint a big ✗ onto your mirror, the chances are that you would never be able to clean it off. Your mum or dad would have to do that properly, wouldn't they?

Can you find out what the word distort means?

27 JANUARY

The plan which God made was a plan that would redeem His creation. The word 'Redeem' means to set free.

God's plan was to set us free from the mark that was put between us and Him because of Adam and Eve's disobedience. However, if we want to set something free there is usually a price to pay. For example, if you want to set a puppy free from a pet shop so that you can take it home - you have to pay for it. The more we want or love a thing, the more we are prepared to pay for it. Well, God loved His creation so much that He was prepared to pay a great price for it.

What does the word Redeem mean?

28 JANUARY

The great price that God was prepared to pay, so that we could be proper friends with Him again, was the price of sending His Son, Jesus, to earth. This was a very big price to pay - more so because Jesus was the only son God had.

Think of it like this - if you had a best friend who wanted very badly to own a puppy and you had two puppies you would probably be willing to give one of them to that friend. It might not be easy, but at least you would still have one puppy. But, imagine if you just had one pup. And you loved it dearly. Could you give that pet away? It would break your heart. I couldn't do that! Well, this is a Person, not a puppy, that we are talking about.

Who was God prepared to send to redeem us?

How many sons did God have?

29 JANUARY

We know that God was prepared to send His only Son, Jesus, to Earth for us. But, that is not all! Jesus would have a job to do on earth to pay for the disobedience which puts the mark between us and God. Jesus would have to die to redeem us.
So, to set His creation free - God sent His Son.
This was God's plan. It was a plan of Salvation. That is a big word, isn't it? But, it is easy to understand - it just means that we escape the punishment. Jesus allowed Himself to take the punishment for disobedience instead of us! This means that the mark is all cleaned away and in order to enjoy God's friendship the way Adam and Eve at first did, we simply accept what Jesus did for us.

> **Can you spell out the word that means to escape punishment?**
>
> S _ _ _ _ _ _ _ _

30 JANUARY

God has written a verse in the Bible which tells the plan of Salvation very clearly. Perhaps after you read it, you could learn it.
It is in the book of John, chapter three, verse sixteen.
'For God so loved the world that He gave His only begotten Son, that whosoever believeth in Him should not perish but have everlasting life.'
This lovely plan of salvation means that you and I can be friends with God and after our lives on earth are over we can also enjoy the Heaven which He has created for us.

> **Why don't you write down as much of the verse in John 3:16 as you can remember?**

31 JANUARY

This is the last day of the first month of the year! You have learnt all about creation and all about salvation. Well, not exactly 'all' - there is much more in the Bible that you can learn about these things.

Why don't you draw a lovely big, bright picture of creation!

17 JANUARY

There are many things that we can learn from creation about God. Let's see if we can find some words which tell us about God that begin with the letter 'G'.

God is GREAT.

He is great because He is powerful. A powerful person has the ability to do great things. Creation is a great thing.

God is GOOD.

When you do something right or get your homework right you are told that is good. If we look at all the things God has created we can see that they are very good.

> **Can you fill in the gaps in this sentence?**
>
> G _ _ is G _ _ _ and G _ _ is G _ _ _ _ .

18 JANUARY

Do you remember looking in the mirror at your reflection? If you had painted a great big black ✗ across the mirror you wouldn't be able to see your reflection properly! Also, if you did paint a big black ✗ across your mirror you probably would be in a lot of trouble! The ✗ would have to be cleaned off before you could see yourself properly, wouldn't it? If that ✗ was left on the mirror everybody else who looked into the mirror would not look right either and it would be your fault!

When we do something wrong it affects other people even if we don't mean it to.

Can you think of something you have done that affected somebody else? May be you didn't put your bike away and somebody fell over it!

19 JANUARY

Adam and Eve did something that they were told not to do and it affected many many people. In fact it even has affected you!
Do you remember the special rule God made for Adam to obey when He put him into the garden?
He told him that he could not eat from the unique tree - the tree of the knowledge of good and evil.
Among all the creatures and animals that God made was the serpent. The serpent was a very crafty creature and one day it decided to have a conversation with Eve. The serpent began the conversation with her. It was a conversation about the trees of the garden.

Can you remember the name of the unique tree ?

The tree of the K _ _ _ _ _ _ _ _ _ of G _ _ _ and E _ _ _

---

20 JANUARY

Eve told the serpent that God did not allow Adam and her to eat from the unique tree. She told him that they could eat from all the other trees except that one. She also told the serpent that they were not allowed even to touch that tree. But, this was not so. God only said that Adam and Eve were not allowed to eat from it. Eve was making the rule harder to obey. Sometimes we make things much harder than they really are! Maybe you are told to tidy your toys away and instead you just shove them all under your bed! Then you are found out and you have to get them all out from under the bed and then put them away. It would have been much easier just to put them away when you were first told ... and nobody would have been cross either!

Why don't you draw a picture of what you think the serpent looked like.

21 JANUARY

Eve told the serpent that GOD had said if they ate from the unique tree they would surely die. When the serpent heard this he decided to lie to Eve. He said that this was not so and told Eve that God didn't want them to eat from the tree because it would make them like gods too. This was a very bad thing for the serpent to say to Eve. God had made this rule for Adam and Eve because He loved them, not because it would stop them being better than they were.

Eve listened to the serpent and broke the rule that God had made and ate the food which she took from the tree. She also gave some of it to Adam.

When Adam and Eve ate this food they both knew they had done what was wrong. They felt shame. Shame is the feeling we have inside when we know when have been bad.

Who did Eve listen to?

Who should Adam and Eve have obeyed?

22 JANUARY

Often when we do something which we know is wrong we want to run away and hide. This is exactly what Adam and Eve did. They tried to hide away from God in among the trees of the garden. When they heard God walking in the garden they tried to avoid Him.

God called Adam and asked him where he was. Adam told God that he was afraid and had hidden himself. God asked Adam if he had eaten from the unique tree. Adam said Eve had given him some of its food and he had eaten it. Eve said the serpent had lied to her about it and she had eaten some of it.

Isn't that just like us! When we have done something wrong we make an excuse by blaming somebody or something else for our own wrong choice.

Why did Adam and Eve hide from God?

23 JANUARY

Can you recall what way the serpent now had to move from place to place?

God, who loved Adam and Eve very much, had now to deal with their disobedience. Firstly God spoke to the serpent who had lied to Eve and changed the serpent into a creature that had now to slide on its belly everywhere it would go.

Then he spoke to Eve who had listened to the serpent and said to her that she would have now to know sorrow and pain in her life.

To Adam he said because he had listened to what Eve had said and not to what God had told him about the unique tree, that he would now have to know hard work in his life. Adam would have to grow his own food, he would have to get rid of thorns and thistles which would now grow among the plants. When we break a rule, often we have a harder rule to obey in its place. For example, if we tell a lie perhaps we are not allowed to play with our favourite toy for a day. It would have been better not to lie than have to do without our favourite toy.

24 JANUARY

Before God sent Adam and Eve out of the garden what did He do for them?

God had now to send Adam and Eve out of their beautiful garden to live. But before He did this He made them coats of skins to clothe them.

Adam and Eve's disobedience meant that some poor animals had to die so that they could be clothed. You see how sad it is when we do what is wrong - other people get hurt just the way these animals were hurt.

All this made God very sad. To guard the beautiful garden God placed at the East of the garden cherubims and a flaming sword which turned around to protect the way to the tree of life.

A cherubim is a winged creature with a human face - it is a bit like an angel.

1 FEBRUARY

We know that God created Heaven. Heaven is described as the abode of God.

An abode is a home or a dwelling place. You have an abode. It is a different dwelling place from your friends, but you like to welcome your friends into your home. Well, Heaven is the home of God and He likes to share His home with other people too. Now, you and I are not always in our home. We go out to school, we go out to play and we go out to visit other places. In this respect God is quite different from us. God is always in Heaven yet He is everywhere else as well. Remember one of the words beginning with "G" that we learnt about God? The word GREAT. Well, God's greatness means that He can do this. There is a very big word that describes how God does this. It is the word OMNIPRESENT. It is easy to say if you divide it into two like so:- 1 OMNI - 2 PRESENT. And it just means that God is present everywhere.

Where is the abode of God?

H _ _ _ _ _

2 FEBRUARY

Heaven is a place and it is quite a different type of place than Earth.

The Earth is a changing place. The weather changes, sometimes it is sunny and sometimes it rains. There are warm days and cold days.

Trees change - in winter they have no leaves, in springtime they have leaves, in summertime they have flowers and in autumn they have fruit.

We change too. We grow bigger. We leave school and start work. Our looks change and the things we do change.

There are many other ways in which the Earth and things on Earth change. Houses are built. Roads are built. Other buildings are knocked down. You can probably think of lots of things around you which change.

Why don't you write down 3 things on Earth which change?

❶

❷

❸

3 FEBRUARY

Heaven is a place which has been specially made ready for us. Jesus said, when he was leaving Earth that He was going to "prepare a place" for us.
When we prepare something we take great care over it. Perhaps you have watched your Mummy prepare for visitors by baking lots of yummy buns and cakes. Perhaps you have seen your Daddy prepare his tools to do a special job. Jesus has taken great care to prepare Heaven for us.

Why don't you draw a picture of what you think Heaven will be like.

4 FEBRUARY

If Jesus has made Heaven ready for us then we must be prepared to go to Heaven.
When your Mummy is busy preparing all those nice things for your visitors to eat – the friends who are coming to visit are getting themselves ready too. They are washing and dressing and putting on their coats so that they are ready to come and visit. Maybe they have even bought a box of chocolates to bring with them.
The way we are made ready for Heaven is by thanking Jesus for coming to Earth and for taking the punishment for our disobedience.

How are we prepared or made ready to go to Heaven?

5 FEBRUARY

What sort of a city is Heaven?

The place of Heaven is a city. This city was built by God for us. It is a beautiful, large, clean city and it has in the centre of it a throne for the Son of God. Because it is a clean city we must be clean to go there. If we weren't clean it would be a bit like eating food with dirty hands. Our dirty hands would spoil the food.

Remember the big ✘ that God had to remove? Well, because Jesus took our punishment for us to remove that ✘, - we are made clean and ready for Heaven.

In order to do this Jesus actually died for us when He was on Earth. After He died and was buried God in His greatness made Jesus come alive again and took Him back home to Heaven. That is where Jesus waits to meet us as He makes everything ready for our arrival.

6 FEBRUARY

Let me tell you some lovely things about Heaven. You already know it is a clean city. Heaven is also a very happy place. I'm sure you have many happy times now - but you also have times when you are not so happy, don't you! In Heaven there will be no sad times at all because Jesus is there to make sure we are not ever sad or lonely or cross or tired or sick.

Heaven has beautiful streets that are made of gold and the stones that the mansions are made from are precious stones, lovely in colour and cut so that the light shines through them. The water in Heaven is perfectly clear and never gets muddy or dirty or smelly.

This is the beautiful place called Heaven.

> **Can you name some of the things which make Heaven a happy and beautiful place?**
>
>

7 FEBRUARY

There is another place which is completely different from Heaven.

It is different because first of all Jesus is not there.

It is different because instead of having light in it like Heaven, it is full of darkness.

Because Jesus is not there and because it is dark this place is a sad and lonely place to be.

The name of this place is Hell.

If God had not loved us and if He had not sent Jesus to Earth to die for us, we would have to go to this ugly place instead of going to Heaven.

This is why it is so important that we know and love Jesus and thank Him for dying for us and for making Heaven such a lovely place for us to go.

Can you remember the name of the place that is not at all like Heaven?

8 FEBRUARY

When Jesus was on Earth he talked a lot about Heaven to the people He met.

He spoke to a man called Nicodemus about Heaven. Nicodemus was a good man who had an important job teaching people many things. Jesus told Nicodemus about Heaven and how he must believe in Him as the Son of God so that he could enjoy Heaven. Just because he was good it did not mean he would be in Heaven. We need to do what Jesus did when He lived on Earth, and tell our friends about Heaven and how they can be sure and go there. They need to thank Jesus for dying for them, and they need to receive Jesus into their heart.

Perhaps you can think over what words you could use to tell your friends about Heaven.

9 FEBRUARY

Jesus spoke about Heaven everywhere He went on Earth. One of the things He said was this - "Blessed are the poor in spirit for theirs is the kingdom of Heaven". Did you know that the word blessed is another word for happy?
So, Jesus is saying that when you know you will be in Heaven it makes you happy.

Are you happy about going to Heaven?

Yes ☐   No ☐

Can you remember what the word blessed means?

H _ _ P _ !

10 FEBRUARY

When Jesus was on Earth He had 12 men who followed Him and who helped Him to do His work. These men were called His Disciples. Jesus taught His Disciples a special prayer. Perhaps you already know the words of this prayer. It is called **THE LORD'S PRAYER**. The very first words of that prayer are about God being in Heaven.
"OUR FATHER WHICH ART IN HEAVEN"
This prayer reminds us that God's home is Heaven. This prayer can be found in the book of the Bible called Matthew. Matthew is the first book of the New Testament. If you find chapter 6 of Matthew and go to verse 9 you can read for yourself all the words of the Lord's Prayer.

Can you find Matthew 6 verse 9 in your Bible?

11 FEBRUARY

Have you ever lost something? It is very easy to lose things. Sometimes it is not our fault that things get lost. Bad people often take things - that is called stealing - and the things they take are lost to us. Sometimes we lose things because they break apart! Perhaps they rust and no longer can be used. Jesus teaches us that in Heaven things like this do not happen. There is no stealing, no rust, no decay. It is much better to look forward to being safe in Heaven than worrying about having lost things hidden away on Earth! Our treasure is all safely kept for us in Heaven.

Can you draw a picture of what you treasure most?

12 FEBRUARY

Jesus knows that we need food and clothes. He knows that it is necessary that we have warmth and shelter. Not only do we need these things but the birds and animals do too. God takes care even of the smallest animal and the tiniest bird. He provides lots of food for them and cozy places for them to live safely. Jesus, when He was living on Earth said that we should not worry about these things because God would provide them for us. He said that all the extra things we need would be given to us but that first of all we should "seek" the kingdom of God. The "kingdom of God" is Heaven. So, Jesus is saying that we must think about Heaven first before we worry about the things of Earth because God will take care of all these things for us.

Do you know what the "kingdom of God" is another name for?

H _ _ _ _ _

13 FEBRUARY

Here is a verse about the kingdom of God which you can learn.

"BUT SEEK YE FIRST THE KINGDOM OF GOD, AND HIS RIGHTEOUSNESS, AND ALL THESE THINGS SHALL BE ADDED UNTO YOU"

It is in the book of Matthew ch. 6. v. 33.

Perhaps you can now fill in the missing spaces of this verse

But _ _ _ _ ye _ _ _ _ _ _
the _ _ _ _ _ _ _ _ of _ _ _ ,
and _ _ _ RIGHTEOUSNESS,
and all these _ _ _ _ _ _
shall be _ _ _ _ _ unto _ _ _ .

Matthew 6: _ _

14 FEBRUARY

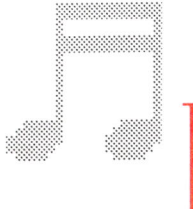

Here are some things that we are going to do in Heaven. We are going to sing!

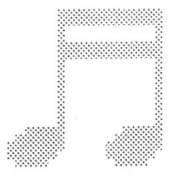

The songs that we will sing will be happy songs that tell how much we love Jesus.

We are going to see Jesus! We can talk to Jesus now in prayer but in Heaven we will be able to meet Him. We are going to be given a crown to wear! Our crowns will be given to us as a prize for obeying Jesus while we lived on Earth.

What do you think your Crown will be like? Why don't you draw a nice picture of it!

15 FEBRUARY

We know that to enter Heaven we must believe Jesus and thank Him for dying for us. We know that Jesus is making Heaven ready for us.
But while we are on Earth there are lots of things that we can do so that we can enjoy our lives here and be ready for Heaven. The first of these things which we can do is have FAITH.
Faith means trust.
We must trust God. Our trust in God is a bit like the foundation of a house. If you build a house and start it wrongly it would fall down and be useless!
If we begin by trusting God in our lives we can add other things to that trust.

What is the word for trust?

F _ _ _ _

16 FEBRUARY

In the New Testament there is a book called Peter - actually there are two books called Peter! First Peter and Second Peter. In Second Peter we find seven things that we can add to our Faith. These are easy to understand and fun to do!
The first is a thing called VIRTUE. VIRTUE simply put means GOOD. It is just as easy to be good as it is to be bad! A good person has courage and strength. God is good so when we have virtue we are like Him. This pleases God as He wants us to be good.

Think about how you can be good and each day do something that will please God.

17 FEBRUARY

When God created us He gave us the ability to learn things. We learn to talk and write. We learn to walk and run. We learn to think and to play and there are many, many other things which we learn. Another word for learning is KNOWLEDGE.

God likes us to also learn about Him. We learn about God in the Bible. The Bible is His book which He has especially written for us.

> **What have you learnt about God? Can you remember the two words which begin with the letter "G" and tell us about God?**
>
> ## God is G_ _ _ _
>
> and
>
> ## God is G_ _ _

18 FEBRUARY

Have you ever seen anyone in a really bad temper? They are so cross they don't even know what they are doing or saying. They probably look very silly indeed! But they might actually scare you too. Well God doesn't like us to lose control of ourselves like that! God never is bad tempered.

Maybe you have seen somebody be greedy and they stuff as much food as they can into their mouths!

Too much temper, too much food - in fact too much of anything isn't good for us!

For example - you might like chocolate but if you ate 20 bars of it you'd be as sick as a horse! But one bar wouldn't harm you.

So, we need to control what we do and what we say and what we eat. There is a big word which describes this - it is the word TEMPERANCE. But, if you think of it as meaning control you will understand it easily enough.

TEMPERANCE   means   C_ _ _ _ _ _ _

19 FEBRUARY

Do you ever get an invitation to a Party and wish it would hurry up and be time to go to it? Maybe you can't wait for school to be over so that you can get outside to play! Do you know what you are not being when you feel like that?

You are not being PATIENT! When we are not patient we are being what is called hasty. When we are hasty we are going too fast and then we make mistakes. Now it is not wise to be too slow either! But being too quick is very silly indeed.

God is patient. He never rushes. He doesn't make mistakes. He has time for us.

We should try hard to be patient because it makes things much, much better.

If you are hasty you are not being

P _ _ _ _ _ _ _ !

20 FEBRUARY

Is there somebody you really want to be like? Maybe you want to be like your brother or sister - maybe you would like to be the same as your best friend or perhaps you wish you were like your Mum or Dad.

Do you wonder why you would like to be the same as somebody else? It is most likely because you love and admire them very much indeed.

God wants us to seek to be like Him. He wants us to imitate Him - to copy Him.

This is called Godliness and it just means GOD-LIKENESS

Think about things which you can do to make you like God - (for example you can be kind to animals)

21 FEBRUARY

God likes us to think of Him as Our Heavenly Father. You have a Father on Earth and you have God as your Father in Heaven. He wants us to think of us all as being a family. When we are part of a family we show special kindness to one another. God wants us to show this kindness to others. The Bible describes this special care for others as brotherly kindness - it just means that we give the sort of kindness to other people that we give to our own brothers and sisters.
That's easy to understand, isn't it?

Who is Our Heavenly Father?

22 FEBRUARY

Of all the things that we can do to be like God and to make ourselves ready for Heaven the greatest is called CHARITY.
Charity means love.
If we are nice to people but don't really mean it we don't really love them. If we are nice on the outside but cross on the inside we don't really love ourselves very much.
Love makes us do things because we really, really want to please and help others. Love means we aren't selfish. It means we take time to do our work and to be kind to others. Love is the gift of God to us and the Bible teaches us that God is love.

Charity is just another word for

L _ _ _

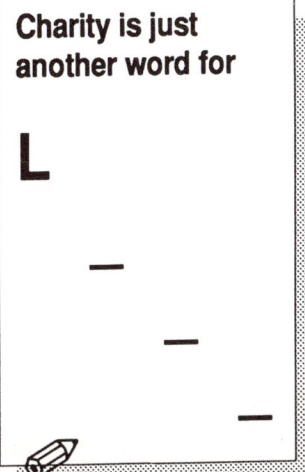

23 FEBRUARY

It seems there are lots of things that we can do to get ready for Heaven. Of course we can't do these all at once. There are lots of things that you have to do each day before you can even go out - you have to get out of bed, you have to wash your face and clean your teeth. You have to make your bed. You have to put on your clothes. You have to put on your shoes. You have to eat your breakfast. Imagine what a mess you would be if you tried to do all these things at once! You would have toothpaste on your toast and shoes in your cornflakes and your PJ's would be half off and half on and your hair would be tossed in every shape! It would be impossible to do all these things at once! God does not expect nor ask us to do everything at once. He just tells us to do a little thing at a time and that way we will learn to become more like Him.

Who do you most want to be like?

24 FEBRUARY

Here are some building blocks. Can you fill in the words which are missing on them? You may need to look back over the past few days to help you. Each one has a clue on it. These are the seven things which we add to our trust in God.

Love is another word for
C _ _ _ _ _ _

B _ _ _ _ _ _ _ _
K _ _ _ _ _ _ _
this shows we care

P _ _ _ _ _ _ _
this means we do not hurry

G _ _ _ _ _ _ _ _
this makes us like God

K _ _ _ _ _ _ _ _
this means to learn

V _ _ _ _ _
this means good

T _ _ _ _ _ _ _ _
this means control

F _ _ _ _
this means trust

25 FEBRUARY

This month we have been learning all about the place called Heaven.

Before any of us ever go to Heaven there is something that will happen to us. We will cease to live on Earth. This means we will die. Death is something that we need not be afraid of because Jesus has promised that He will never ever leave us. He said "I will never leave thee nor forsake thee". This means we can not ever be left alone. When He tells us this we trust Him.

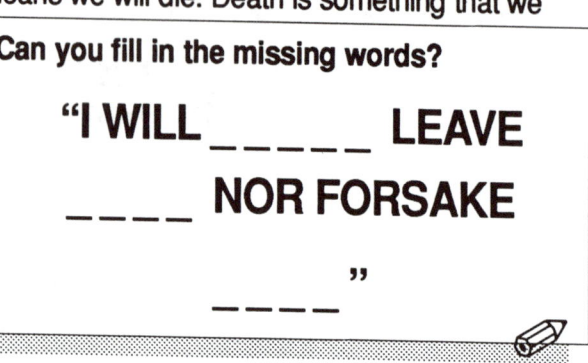

Can you fill in the missing words?

"I WILL _ _ _ _ _ _ LEAVE _ _ _ _ NOR FORSAKE _ _ _ _"

26 FEBRUARY

It might seem a bit hard to understand what happens when we die. We no longer live on Earth. Instead we live in Heaven. I suppose it is a bit like going from one room in your house into another room. You can't be seen through the wall! But everyone knows you have gone into that room and that you are there.

From Earth we cannot see into Heaven. We cannot see the people who are already there but we know that Heaven is ready for us and that God is waiting to meet us there.

So death is just like a doorway which opens into Heaven.

Can you think of anyone you know who will be in Heaven with you?

27 FEBRUARY

Death could have been a very awful thing if Jesus did not conquer it for us. Conquer means He overcame it. Do you know how He did this? He came alive again after He died. If Jesus had not risen from the dead, death would have won! But the power of Jesus was stronger than the power of death and He claimed for us eternal life. Eternal life means we can live for ever with Him in Heaven after our earthly life ends. The Bible tells us that eternal life is a present or a gift to us from God. What an amazing gift!

Have you accepted this wonderful gift from God?

28 FEBRUARY

Let's see what you can remember about Heaven?

★ Heaven is a **P** _ _ _ _ _ .

★ Heaven has light and happiness but Hell has **D** _ _ _ _ _ _ _ _ and is a **L** _ _ _ _ _ _ place to be.

★ In Heaven   we will **S** _ _ _
                we will be **H** _ _ _ _
                we will wear a **C** _ _ _ _ _

★ Jesus has a **T** _ _ _ _ _ _ in the centre of Heaven.

★ Heaven is very beautiful. It's streets are made of **G** _ _ _ .

29 FEBRUARY

This is the last day of the second month of the year! You have learnt about the place called Heaven.

Here is a space for you to draw a lovely picture of what you imagine Heaven will be like.

1 MARCH

How do you make friends with someone? You talk to them, don't you. Talking to people we meet means that we get to know lots of things about them and they also get to know things about us. We ask them questions - they give us answers. They ask us questions and we answer their questions. Can you imagine trying to get to know somebody who didn't talk to you? It would be impossible! Jesus wants to know us and the best way for us to get to know Him is to talk to Him. Jesus has made a special means of talking for us to use when we want to speak to Him. It is called prayer.

Do you talk to Jesus in prayer?

What sort of things do you say to Him?

2 MARCH

Jesus taught his 12 Disciples how to pray. The way He did this was by teaching them a prayer. These are the words which He taught them. They are easy to learn and simple to understand. You probably know some of them already - but, if you don't it won't take you long to be able to say this prayer all by yourself. This prayer is called The Lord's Prayer.

Our Father which art in Heaven, hallowed be thy name. Thy kingdom come, thy will be done on earth as it is in heaven. Give us this day our daily bread and forgive us our trespasses, as we forgive those who trespass against us, and lead us not into temptation but deliver us from evil, for thine is the kingdom, the power and the glory, for ever and ever, Amen.

Do you remember what this prayer is called?

The

L _ _ _ ' _

P _ _ _ _ _

3 MARCH

The Lord's Prayer is really a pattern for other prayers. Do you know what a pattern is? A pattern is a design which can be used to make other things. The things which are made from a pattern are not all exactly the same but they are very similar. For example - perhaps you have to wear a uniform to school. All the other boys and girls in your school have to wear the same uniform. But some of them are tall, some are small, some are plump, some are fat, some are skinny. Some have great long legs, some have short legs. Some have broad backs, some have narrow shoulders! Goodness me, what an assortment of shapes all the boys and girls in your school are! So the uniform which you all wear even though it is the same uniform, has to be made specially to fit each boy and each girl - otherwise nobody's would fit properly and you would all look plain daft!
If that was the case the whole point of having a uniform would be ruined because a uniform is made to keep everyone neat and tidy.

> **Can you fill in the missing word in this sentence?**
>
> **The Lord's Prayer is really a P _ _ _ _ _ for other prayers.**

4 MARCH

Just as you have to have your school uniform or in fact, any of your clothes, chosen so as they really fit you so too does Jesus like us to talk to Him about things that really matter to us. I mean, it would be a bit silly for you to pray that you would be better from the chicken pox if you didn't have chicken pox! On the other hand it would be very foolish for us to not talk to God about things that we have need of. When you need or want something you feel free to talk to your Mum and Dad and ask them for the things you need and want.
After all you wouldn't bother asking your dog if you needed a new pair of shoes! You'd ask your parents because they would be able to do something about it.
God wants us to freely talk to him with as much ease as we talk to our parents because He is our Heavenly Father.

> **Can we talk freely to our Heavenly Father in prayer the way we talk to our Mum and Dad?**

5 MARCH

Let's see if we can find the pattern in The Lord's Prayer that will help us to know how to pray.
Can you recall the first two words of The Lord's Prayer?
They are "Our Father".
This shows us that our prayers are made to our Heavenly Father because it is He who hears and answers our prayers.
If you were thirsty and went into a shop to buy a can of drink and there were lots of people in the shop you would ask the shop keeper for the drink you wanted to buy. You wouldn't just open the door into the shop and yell "I want a drink!" and you wouldn't just go up to any of the people and give them the money for your drink! That would be very silly indeed. You would go directly to the counter to get what you needed.
So the first part of the pattern is easy to remember, isn't it? It starts with the letter F and F is for Father. Our prayers are made to our Heavenly Father.

Can you fill in the missing letters?

_ is for _ A _ _ E _

6 MARCH

F for Father is the first part of the prayer pattern. The second part begins with the letter A. A is for adore. When we adore somebody we love them very, very much. When we love somebody we tell them that we love them and how much we love them.
Don't you feel special when your Mum or Dad tells you how much they love you? And I'm sure you like to tell your Mum and Dad how much you love them too. The love which you have for your Mum and Dad is a different sort of love than you have for your toys.
You might say that you love your bike but you know that means something different than the way you love your Mum and Dad!
The word Adore describes the special love we have for God. God wants us to tell Him how much we love Him when we talk to Him each day.
A is for Adore and it is the second part of the prayer pattern.

What word in the prayer pattern begins with A?

A _ _ _ _

7 MARCH

When we do something wrong we have to own up to it! We all do wrong things and when we do it is best to admit that we have been bad. If we don't, we have to do more wrong to hide the truth. We have to tell lies. Do you know what lies are?

Lies are filthy wee bugs that turn us into nasty, rotten, ugly people. These sort of people are called liars - ugh! Don't you hate lies! Wouldn't you hate to become one of those people all full of dirty wee lie bugs that breed and breed inside them and then crawl out of their mouths and ears and noses and make them very ugly indeed!

Well, when we do something wrong and say that we have done it we are doing what is called confessing. Confessing means telling. When we talk to God in prayer we Confess or tell Him what we have done that is not good or honest or nice. In a way we are telling God on ourselves. When we tell God what we have done wrong then he can forgive us and help us to be good.

C is for Confess and is the third part of the prayer pattern.

Confess means to

T _ _ _

8 MARCH

The fourth part of the prayer pattern begins with T and it is a very important part indeed because it makes the pattern beautiful.

What colour is the door into your house. Is it red? Maybe it is green - or blue or perhaps it has pretty glass or a nice shiny varnish over the wood. Now that door would work just as well if it had no colourful paint on it or no pretty glass or no nice shiny varnish, wouldn't it? It would still open and shut, keep the rain out and let people come inside your house. But doesn't it look much nicer with bright paint, or pretty glass, or nice shiny varnish?

The last part of the prayer pattern is T for Thanks. When we pray we must remember to be thankful. We must thank God for the things He has given to us - even the little things. We should thank Him for caring for us each day by giving us food and drink. God will let us talk to Him whether we do this or not - but it is a better friendship if we are thankful for all He does. We should also thank the people we love who do kind things for us every single day.

T is for Thanks.

Thanks in prayer makes our prayers B _ A _ _ _ F _ L

9 MARCH

We have learnt the prayer pattern which Jesus showed His Disciples by teaching them The Lord's Prayer. If all our prayers include these things they will make God very happy. The prayer pattern spells a word. When you fill in the gaps below you will find the word!

The Prayer Pattern

☐ is for **Father** to whom we pray.

☐ is for **Adore** which means love.

☐ is for **Confess** which means we tell our wrong and are forgiven.

☐ is for **Thanks** which makes our prayers beautiful.

Did you find the word? Of course you did! The word is **FACT**. If you remember this small word each letter will remind you of the things that are in the prayer pattern.

10 MARCH

You will find that the more you talk to God in prayer the more you will get to know Him. Who would you say knows you the best? It is probably your Mum and Dad or your brothers and sisters. But whoever it is who knows you the best - knows you because you talk to them every single day. There are lots of people whom you know but you don't know them very well. Perhaps just enough to say hello to, maybe just well enough to play a game with every so often. But the people you know best you can talk to easily, can't you? If you had something wonderful happen - you'd tell them first or if you had something sad happen you would want to be with them and nobody else. Also if something or somebody made you scared - you could tell them and they would help you. Our Heavenly Father wants very much to be our best friend. So, when you are happy - tell Him! When you are sad - tell Him. When you are afraid - tell Him. He will be happy with you, he will help you to not be so sad and He will protect you from fear.

> Can you think of the people who know you best?
>
> And can you think of the people you know best?

11 MARCH

When God was gathering together all the true stories which are in the Bible for us to read, He put an awful lot of examples about prayer into it. This shows how important God views prayer to be. After all - if it was of no use to us He wouldn't have bothered to go to all that trouble. God doesn't tell us in the Bible to go and paint our teeth green! He doesn't tell us to walk on our elbows! He doesn't tell us to eat carpet! You can do all these things if you really want to but you'd look very foolish and you'd be very sick. But God does tell us that we should pray and he tells us that is what makes Him very happy indeed. In the book named Proverbs we read this sentence "The prayer of the upright is His delight". This is an easy sentence to understand. It means the prayers of God's children make Him most happy.

> Do you think you could learn this sentence?
>
> **'THE PRAYER OF THE UPRIGHT IS HIS DELIGHT'**
>
> Proverbs 15 vs. 8

12 MARCH

God's children are special to Him. A precious thing is of great value - in fact, it is of such value that it could not be priced! ! That is how your parents feel about you - they would never sell you because there would never be enough money to make it worth their while.

God feels exactly that way about His creation - but did you know that even more than this He loves His children!

God's children are all the people in the world who believe in Him. That's very simple isn't it!

The very first thing which you must do is to tell God that you believe in Him. You need to tell Him that you are glad He sent His Son Jesus to take away the big black ✗ that Adam put between us and God. When we do this God accepts us as His own children and makes us His very own precious belonging which He will never ever give away!

> Why don't you think about asking God to make you one of His special children. Maybe you already have asked Him to do this - well, then you don't need to do it again. You are already His, aren't you!

13 MARCH

When God's children talk to Him in prayer He hears them. Wouldn't it be very annoying if you talked to your Mum and Dad and they didn't listen! Your Mum and Dad take time to listen to you.

When God hears our prayers He answers them. Now that doesn't mean that He always says "yes." Sometimes He has to say "no" and sometimes He makes us wait a little while or even a long while before He can give us what we are asking Him for. That's not hard to understand now is it? Think about it like this - does your Mummy answer all your questions by saying yes!? Sometimes she has to say no because it would not be good for you to have it. Maybe you asked if you could have a penknife and she said no because you might hurt yourself with it. Sometimes your Daddy tells you that you have to wait for something you want. Maybe you want to use the hedge cutters but you couldn't use them now. However, when you are older he would let you use them. You see, God treats us much the same way as this. He is glad to give us things that are good for us but He keeps from us things that would hurt us.

Do you know why God sometimes has to say "no" to us?

14 MARCH

Moses was the friend of God. He was one of God's children and there were many things that Moses asked God for and which God gave Him. But Moses was just like you and me. He didn't always do what he was told! When we disobey it often means that we cannot have something that otherwise we would have had. Let's pretend you like to go ice skating. One day your Dad promises to take you skating. But let's also pretend that before the time comes to go skating you go into the garage, open your Daddy's tool box and take out his best screwdriver, then forget where you put it and it is lost! Your Dad is very cross and because you disobeyed him, he decides not to take you skating. You would be very disappointed wouldn't you? But you know that it's not your Dad's fault - it is your own fault for not obeying him. So we can understand why it is important to obey because things that are promised to us can be taken from us if we do not obey.

Can you imagine what Moses looked like?

15 MARCH

Moses was given the job of leading the people of Israel into a new country which God had promised them. In Egypt they had been treated very badly. Because God loved them He made it possible for them to escape. God made Moses their leader and like all the other people he was looking forward to arriving in their new country. But Moses disobeyed God. One day when the people of Israel were on their journey from Egypt to Canaan (that was the name of the new country to which they were going) they had to travel across a desert called Zin. Now, as you know, there is no water in a desert and all the people started to yap and moan and complain to Moses and his brother Aaron.

Who should you steer clear of?

M _ _ _ _ _ _ !

Isn't it awful when people moan to you! Do you ever moan? Moaning is a bad thing to do because it spreads! If you ever meet somebody who is a moaner keep away from them or you will catch the moaning disease! Poor Moses - he was stuck with a bunch of people who had the moaning disease!

16 MARCH

Moses and Aaron realised that they couldn't shut up all the moaners. The only thing that would cure them from the moaning disease was the water that they wanted. So they talked to God about the problem and God told Moses what to do.

He said to gather all the people who were moaning together around a big rock which was in the desert. Then Moses was to speak to the rock and God would create water and let it come out of the rock. So Moses and his brother did this. Of course Moses was annoyed with the people because they were moaning and he said cross words to them - he called them rebels! Do you know what a rebel is? A rebel is a person who doesn't like his leader and all these people were behaving as though they didn't like Moses and blamed him for the fact that there was no water. So Moses said "Right - you rebels! - must we fetch you water out of this rock?" and he lifted his stick and hit the rock! Oh, oh!! That's not what God told him to do.

God told Moses to

S _ _ _ _ _ to the rock

17 MARCH

When Moses hit that rock a great whack with his stick do you know what happened? Did it squeal in pain? I don't think so! Did it hit him back? - No, it didn't do that either! When he hit it, gallons and gallons and gallons of water gushed out of it! There was so much water that every single person and every single animal had enough to drink. But God was annoyed at Moses for hitting the rock. God told him to speak, not to hit the rock. Because Moses disobeyed, God told him and his brother that they would never enter into the new country which He had promised to give to all His people. Can you see how important it is to do what is right? When Moses did what was right God was able to say "yes" to him, but when he did what was wrong, God had to say "no" to him.

> God was annoyed at Moses because he
>
> H _ _ the rock

18 MARCH

God would rather say "yes" to us than say "no" to us. There was a man called Elijah who asked God to stop the rain and it did stop raining! That was a strange thing to ask God to do, wasn't it? Elijah was a very interesting person who talked to God every day in prayer. This made him a close friend of God's and God often helped him. When Elijah asked God for it to stop raining it was to show to the people among whom Elijah lived that God was the only true God. Some of the people Elijah knew worshipped other gods who had no power to do anything. These people prayed to statues and images. Now a statue or an image cannot do anything. It might look very nice or it might be very big in size and seem strong - but statues can't actually move or speak, let alone change things. It's a bit like you looking at your bicycle and telling it to go for a ride! Your bike couldn't just ride off on its own, now could it? But if you get on to it, because you have the ability to balance it and push the pedals and steer it, it can be taken wherever you want to take it. Well - God has the power and the ability to answer our prayers. He is not like a statue -He is real.

> Can you fill in the missing word?
>
> God is R _ _ _

19 MARCH

When Elijah asked God for the rain to stop - do you know how long it stopped raining for? An hour? No! A day? No! It stopped raining for three years and six months! And do you know that even when God showed His power for as long a time as that - there were still people who didn't believe God was real! Now that's plain stubborn, isn't it? If you are stubborn it means that you are wilful, you don't easily change your mind. There are times when we need to be strong-willed but if we never ever change our minds about anything that makes us stubborn in a way that hurts us. It also means that we can hurt other people too. Think about all the people to whom Elijah was trying to show the real God. He asked that there be no rain so that God's power to even stop the rain falling showed them who the real God was. Well, when there was no rain even the people who did believe in the real God had to go without rain as well. So you see, when we are stubborn other people are affected by our stubbornness too!

How long did God stop the rain from falling for Elijah?

_ years and _ months

20 MARCH

After three years and six months Elijah asked God if He would allow it to start raining. Again God showed that He was able to control the rain and He let it start raining!

But Elijah did not always get what he wanted when he prayed because he didn't always ask God for things that were good for him. One time he asked God if He would let him die! Imagine asking God for something like that! God knew it wouldn't be good for Elijah to die so He kept him alive. Elijah wanted to die because he was afraid of a wicked queen. God had to teach Elijah that when he was afraid of something the answer wasn't to die! But it was to realise that God was bigger and stronger than the thing he was afraid of. Our Heavenly Father wants us to let Him know when we are afraid because He can keep us safe and help us not to be frightened. In 1st Kings chapter 19 you can read this story about Elijah.

Can you find the name of the Queen of whom Elijah was afraid?

Queen J_ _ _ _ _ _

21 MARCH

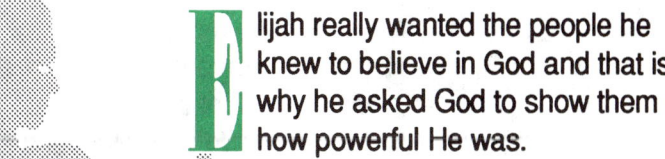

Elijah really wanted the people he knew to believe in God and that is why he asked God to show them how powerful He was. There are lots of ways that we can show people that we know that God is a real God. We can be thoughtful about others. Thoughtfulness is a big word isn't it? It has 14 letters in it! But it isn't a hard word to understand. It simply means that we think about other people and do nice things for them. Maybe your Mummy had a friend who was sick and in hospital and she took flowers to them - that is thoughtfulness. Maybe your Daddy got in from work early and put dinner on to cook - that is thoughtfulness. When we are thoughtful we are like God because God thinks about us and does lots of helpful things for us. When we talk to God in prayer we should ask Him to help us to be thoughtful so that we can show other people how good God is to us and to them.

Can you fill in the gaps?

God is very T _ _ _ _ _ _ _ _ _ to us.

22 MARCH

When we have something or know something that is very good, we like to share it. We like to share our toys with our friends. We like to share our sweets with our Mum and Dad. We like to share lots of things. People who don't share are selfish. That means they want everything for themselves! That also makes them greedy, and greedy people aren't very pleasant people at all. In fact they are nasty people. Another word for 'selfish' is the word 'mean'. I would hate to be called mean, wouldn't you? God isn't a mean, selfish God. He is kind and loving and generous. Look at all the things He gives to us every single day! Fresh air, food to eat, pure water to drink, healthy bodies, nice clothes, and a lovely house to live in. God wants us to also share His kindness and love with others. One way is by sharing things with others. Another way is by telling our friends that God loves them too.

Another word for 'Selfish is the word

M _ _ _

51

23 MARCH

It might seem to you that there are an awful lot of things to remember when we pray. But prayer isn't a hard thing for you to do at all! Do you find it hard to talk to your Mum and Dad or your friends? Not at all! In fact you don't really have to think over every single conversation you have - goodness me if you did that, you wouldn't have time to talk at all!! Well, when you talk to God it should be as easy and straightforward as talking to your Mum and Dad. You can talk to your Mum and Dad at any time, can't you? You can talk to them about anything, can't you? And you can certainly talk to them anywhere - you don't have to be in your garden to talk to them! You don't have to be sitting on the roof to talk to them! You don't have to get under the kitchen table to talk to them, do you?! You just talk to them wherever you are. At home, in the garden, on holidays, in the car - anywhere at all. We can talk to God wherever we are.

> We can talk to God at
> **ANY T _ _ _**
>
> We can talk to God about
> **ANYT _ _ _ G**
>
> We can talk to God
> **ANYW _ _ _ E**

24 MARCH

We can talk to God at any time.
King David often talked to God in the morning time. Daniel talked to God in the morning time, in the afternoon and in the evening time. King David also talked to God at night - in fact even in the middle of the night if David woke up he would talk to God.
Just like these people we can talk to God at any time. This is very important because it means that we are free to talk to God just when we need to. It would be pretty awful if we had to wait until a certain time of the day before we could talk to our Mum and Dad! Well, thankfully we don't have to wait until a certain time of day to talk to God. We can say "Good morning" to Him, we can have a talk with Him at lunch time and we can say "Good night" to Him as well - and we can talk to Him at any time in between too!

> We can talk to God at any
> **T _ _ _**

25 MARCH

We can talk to God about anything. God is interested in everything about us. He wants us to talk to Him about anything we want to tell Him, or ask Him for, or thank Him for.

Remember Elijah? He talked to God about rain. Daniel talked to God about lions. David talked to God about giants.

So you see - there is nothing at all about which we cannot talk to God.

We can talk to God about any

ANYT_ _ _ _

26 MARCH

We can talk to God anywhere. Did you know that you don't have to be in Church to talk to God? Did you know that you don't have to kneel down to talk to God? Of course you do and can talk to God in Church and you can kneel down to pray if you like to do that. It isn't even necessary to close your eyes when you talk to God in prayer. The reason why we close our eyes is to help us to think about God because when we aren't looking at other things we can think better about what we are saying to Him.

Can you think about some places people were when they talked to God?

Adam was in the garden set in Eden when he talked to God. David was in a battle field fighting Goliath when he talked to God. Elijah was under a tree when he talked to God, and think about Jonah! He was in the belly of a whale when he talked to God. I don't suppose you have ever been in a whale's belly to say your prayers!!

We can talk to God

ANYW_ _ _ E

27 MARCH

Let's see if you can complete this puzzle.

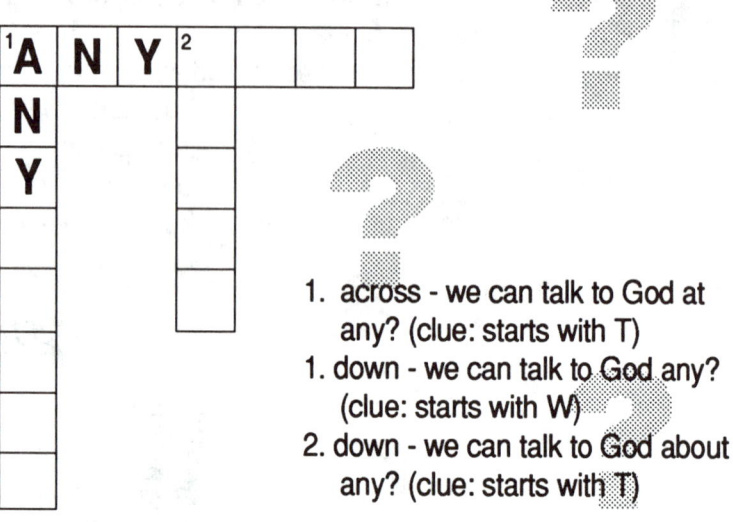

1. across - we can talk to God at any? (clue: starts with T)
1. down - we can talk to God any? (clue: starts with W)
2. down - we can talk to God about any? (clue: starts with T)

28 MARCH

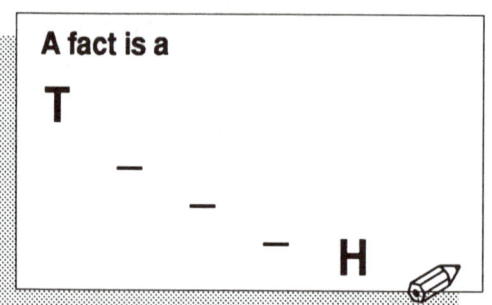

A fact is a
T _ _ _ H

Do you remember the prayer pattern? The word which reminds us of the prayer pattern is the word FACT.

F is for Father
A is for Adore
C is for Confess
T is for Thanks

A fact is a truth. When somebody tells you a fact they are telling you something which is true. Here are some examples of facts.
It is a fact that people have two legs!
It is a fact that people do not have four arms!
It is a fact that grass is green!
It is a fact that apples are not blue!
It is a fact that dogs bark!
It is a fact that cows do not bark!
There are lots of facts in the Bible that God tells us about prayer.

29 MARCH

It is a fact that God hears our prayers.
Did you realise that God isn't deaf! If God was deaf He wouldn't hear our prayers. How do we know God hears our prayers? Well, tell me how do you know your Mum or Dad hears you?

You know because they answer you and you know because quite often they tell you that they can hear you!

God tells us in the Bible that He hears our prayers. The way God tells us this is by explaining to us that He keeps his ears open to hear us. If you cover your ears you are closing out the sound. God never puts His hands over His ears when His children talk to Him in prayer.

Can you complete this sentence?

It is a F _ _ _ that God

H _ _ R _ our prayers

30 MARCH

It is also a fact that God answers our prayers.

How do you know that the things you ask your parents for or that the things you ask your parents about are answered? You know because there is evidence. Do you know what evidence is?

Evidence is proof. For example if you fall and cut your knee the evidence or proof that you fell is seen by your cut knee. If you were to stick your hands into a bucket of purple paint the proof that you did this would be your purple hands!

So, when God answers our prayers we can see the proof for ourselves.

Look all around you and you will see proof of God's answers to your prayers! You should think every day about all the prayers God has answered for you today.

Can you complete this sentence?

It is a F _ _ _ that God

A _ _ W _ _ _ our prayers

31 MARCH

This is the last day of the month of March. March is the third month of the year. This month you have been learning lots of things about prayer.

There is another lovely fact about prayer that you should know.

It is the fact that Jesus prays for us! Isn't it nice when somebody else asks for something on your behalf? Well, Jesus, God's Son, talks to God His Father and asks Him for the things He knows we need.

Jesus is like an older brother who likes to look after us and talk to our Heavenly Father for us. When you pray remember that Jesus is praying for you. He goes to God on your behalf!!

> **Fill in the gaps in this sentence**
>
> Jesus P _ _ _ _ for us!

1 APRIL

The Bible is divided into TWO main parts. These two parts are called **The Old Testament** and **The New Testament**.
The number two is used by God many times. He used it when He created us. He gave us two arms and two legs. He gave us two hands and two feet. He gave us two eyes and two ears. He didn't give us two noses! But He did give us two nostrils in our nose. He didn't give us two mouths and isn't it a good job that He didn't for can you imagine how hard it would be to talk with two mouths!!
God also created two types of people - a man and a woman. Can you remember what God created on day two? He created Heaven. The number two reminds us of all these things.

Find where the number 2 goes in these sentences?

There are ☐ parts in the Bible, The Old Testament and The New Testament.

God created ☐ types of people - a man and a woman.

On day ☐ God made Heaven.

2 APRIL

The two parts of the Bible are divided into books.
The Old testament has **39** books.
The New Testament has **27** books.
The Old Testament begins with a book called Genesis and ends with a book called Malachi.
The New Testament begins with a book called Matthew and ends with a book called Revelation.
Altogether there are **66** books in the Bible!

Circle the right answer:

The Old Testament has **45** or **23** or **39** books

The New Testament has **39** or **20** or **27** books.

Altogether there are **10** or **76** or **66** books in the Bible.

3 APRIL

God made ONE way for us to go to Heaven. That ONE way was by sending His Son, Jesus, to take away the big black ✘ of our sins. There aren't two ways to Heaven! There aren't six ways to Heaven! There is just the ONE way to Heaven.

Do you remember that on day ONE of creation God made LIGHT? Jesus is the light of the world. Just as the light shows us where we can go, Jesus shows us the way to Heaven. He shows us that He took our punishment for the ✘ of our wrong doing and made it possible for us to be the friends of God.

> **Find where the number 1 fits in these sentences:**
>
> There is ☐ way to Heaven.
>
> On day ☐ of creation God made the light.
>
> Jesus is the ☐ person who took away our sins.

4 APRIL

When Jesus died for us there were THREE crosses put on the hill called Golgotha. Jesus was hung on the middle cross and on either side of Him there was a thief. These two men were being punished for their own wrong doing which was stealing. Jesus was being punished for our wrong doing.

After Jesus died He was buried but on day THREE He came alive again because He was stronger than death.

The number THREE should remind us of what Jesus did for us. On day THREE when He rose from the dead He had completed the job which God had sent Him to earth to do. There are lots of times when God uses the number three in the Bible. The three wise men, who visited Jesus when He was a baby, brought Him three gifts. There were three men thrown into the fiery furnace - you can find the story about them in the book of Daniel chapter THREE in your Bible.

On day ☐ Jesus rose from the dead!

5 APRIL

Here is a little song that has lots of numbers in it
TWO little fishes
FIVE loaves of bread
5 thousand people
By Jesus were fed
This is what happened
When ONE little lad
Gladly gave Jesus all that he had!

ONE lonely widow
TWO coins small
Jesus was watching
When she gave her all
And Jesus said
That His heart was made glad
That she had given all that she had.

The two stories which this song tells us about can be found in the Bible. The first is in the book of Mark, chapter 8. The second is in the book of Mark, chapter 12. **Why don't you find them and read all about them!**

6 APRIL

Do you know how many days there are in a week? There are SEVEN days in one week. One of those days has been created by God for us to have a rest from work. That is the day which we call Sunday. There are SEVEN colours in the rainbow. God made the first rainbow and put it into the sky as a promise to Noah that the world would never again be destroyed by a flood. The promise of the rainbow with its seven colours is told for us in the book of Genesis chapter 9. **Why don't you find it in your Bible.** Do you know what the SEVEN colours of the rainbow are? They are Red, Orange, Yellow, Blue, Green, Indigo and Violet.

An easy way to remember the 7 colours of the rainbow is to think of a wee man called Roy B. Giv. If you learn this wee man's name each letter will remind you of a colour! R for red, O for orange, Y for yellow etc. This is a fun way to learn all the colours of the rainbow!

7 APRIL

When God created us He knew that it was important that we had guidelines to help us to live. When you go out onto the road in a motor car or on your bike there are rules which you must follow if you don't want to have an accident. Of course you can just ignore these rules but you will be very sorry if you do! You would have a very nasty accident if you didn't bother stopping at the red light wouldn't you!

God has given us just 10 rules which we should obey. These 10 rules are the 10 commandments. God put the 10 commandments onto two tablets of stone. On one half He wrote the first 5 commandments on the other half He wrote the last 5 commandments.

The number 10 should remind us of the 10 commandments.

Fill in the missing numbers.

God has given us ☐ rules to teach us how to live. These rules are called the ☐ commandments.

8 APRIL

When Jesus lived on Earth he chose 12 men to be His helpers. These 12 men were called His Disciples.
A Disciple is a person who follows.
The 12 Disciples followed Jesus.

Can you answer these questions?

How many Disciples did Jesus have? ☐

How many were good? ☐

ONE Disciple betrayed Jesus. His name was

J_ D _ S

Of the 12 Disciples there was 1 who betrayed Jesus. This Disciple was called Judas. If you betray somebody you let them down in a major way. Judas showed the Roman soldiers who Jesus was so that they could take Him away, judge Him and then crucify Him.

Of the 12 Disciples only 11 were true followers of Jesus. Jesus wants us to be like the 11 good Disciples.

9 APRIL

When Judas betrayed his friend Jesus, he did that job for the Roman soldiers. The Roman soldiers paid him to do it. They paid him 30 pieces of silver. Imagine betraying your friend for money! When we are a true friend to somebody we wouldn't take money from someone else money to tell mean things on them. We wouldn't take money from somebody else to stop being their friend. In fact we would be very cross with the person who tried to buy from us our friendship. Judas was prepared to take 30 coins from the Roman soldiers to sell his friend Jesus to them. The number 30 reminds us of the sad story about Judas who sold Jesus to be crucified.

> Can you fill in the missing number and letters?
>
> Jesus was sold for ☐ pieces of silver to the soldiers by J _ D _ _

10 APRIL

The number 33 tells us how many years Jesus lived on the Earth. Jesus was 33 years of age when He returned to Heaven. During his 33 years on Earth Jesus did many things. He did so many things that the Bible tells us that if they were all written down the world would not be able to hold all the books that they would make! So, there is no number which could tell us the many things which Jesus did! But the number 33 tells us what age Jesus was when He returned to Heaven.

> Jesus lived ☐ years on Earth.

11 APRIL

When God caused the whole world to be destroyed by a flood, He let it rain for 40 days and 40 nights. By the time all that rain had stopped even the highest mountain was covered by water. The world was just one huge swimming pool and the only people alive were Noah and his wife, and his 3 sons and their wives. That equals 8 people. Of course there were lots of animals in the Ark with Noah and his family but there were only 8 people chosen by God to survive the flood. The story of the flood and how Noah built his great Ark is found in the book of Genesis. It starts at chapter 6 and it is a great story to read.

> There were only ☐ people saved from the flood

12 APRIL

The number 99 is a big number, isn't it? It would take you quite a long time to count to 99! 99 is just one number short of 100. Jesus told a story about the number 99 when He was living on Earth.

The story was about a shepherd who owned 100 sheep. The shepherd discovered one day that one of his sheep was missing and instead of having 100 sheep he only had 99 sheep. Because the shepherd cared for his sheep and was worried about the one sheep that was lost he searched and searched until he found it. When he found it, he lifted it up and carried it back to the 99 sheep which were all together so that it was safe again. Jesus said, at the end of His story, that even when just ONE person was sorry for their sins that everyone in Heaven was very happy. The ONE sheep which was lost was so important to the shepherd that he took time to look for it even though he still had 99 others which were safe.

Each one of us is important to Jesus our Shepherd.

> How many sheep were safe? ☐
>
> How many sheep were lost? ☐

13 APRIL

Here is a quiz. Can you fill in the missing numbers! Remember there are lots more numbers in the Bible than just these ones! Look out for them when you are reading your Bible.

- ★ God has made ☐ way to Heaven.
- ★ God created ☐ people, a man and a woman.
- ★ Jesus rose from the dead ☐ days after He was buried.
- ★ There were ☐ men in the fiery furnace.
- ★ God wrote ten rules called the ☐ commandments.
- ★ There are ☐ colours in the rainbow.
- ★ Jesus had ☐ Disciples.
- ★ Judas sold Jesus for ☐ pieces of silver.
- ★ Jesus lived ☐ years on Earth.
- ★ There were ☐ people in the Ark.
- ★ The shepherd had ☐ sheep, ☐ were safe and ☐ was lost.

14 APRIL

Wouldn't the world be a very dull place if God hadn't made any colours! Imagine if there was no colour blue for the sky! The colour blue should remind us of Heaven. Do you know why the sea is blue? The sea is blue because it reflects the colour of the sky. That is what we should do too. We should reflect or show to all our friends how happy we are to be going to Heaven!

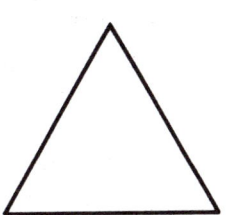

Can you colour this shape blue?

15 APRIL

The grass is green. Most of the plants and trees which grow around us have lots of the colour green on them. In fact, if they don't have green it usually means they have something wrong with them.

Trees have green leaves. Flowers have green leaves and stems. Wheat and barley are green before they ripen and are ready to be harvested. When trees and plants are healthy and have plenty of water to help them grow they are nice and green. If it is hot and if there is not enough water the grass and plants and trees lose their fresh green colour and start to wither. The colour green reminds us of growth. We should let our knowledge about Jesus and our love for our Heavenly Father grow each day. We can do this by reading our Bible, by talking to God in prayer and by doing what is right. Then we will be like nice, bright green grass - fresh and beautiful to look at.

Colour this spot green.

Green reminds us of

GR _ W _ H

16 APRIL

Remember the big black ✘ of our sins which Jesus came to take away for us? Well, doesn't the colour black remind us of darkness? When Jesus takes away the blackness of our sins He leaves whiter than snow. If something is as white as snow, it is very bright to look at. The white snow covers everything when it falls. It doesn't just say as it is falling "mmm now, I think I shall cover that tree but not cover the one beside it! And I think I will cover just six blades of grass in that garden and not bother covering the rest!"

Jesus cleanses us from the Black ✘ of our sin and leaves us W _ _ _ _ _ than snow.

Oh no - the snow covers it all and leaves everywhere looking pure white! When Jesus takes away our sins He takes them all away! He doesn't just take one or two away, he doesn't just take 20 or 30 away. He takes them all away! Every last bit of the big black ✘ is removed. The colour white reminds us of how clean Jesus makes us.

17 APRIL

The first colour of the rainbow begins with the letter R. It is the colour red. When Jesus died on the cross He shed His precious Blood so that He could cleanse us from our sins. Without the blood of Jesus being shed there would have been no way that our sins could have been washed away. Our sins were so dark and black that it took the Blood of Jesus to remove their stain from us. A stain is a mark. Jesus loved us very much - enough to die for us.

The colour red is one of the brightest and most noticeable colours that God has created. He has put little splashes of it everywhere throughout His creation. When we see red we are reminded of the precious Blood of Jesus which washes away our sins and makes us ready for Heaven. There are verses in the Bible which teach us about the Blood of Jesus. One of these is found in the book of 1 John, chapter 1 and verse 7. It says, "the Blood of Jesus Christ, God's Son, cleanseth us from all sin."

> Why not look up I John chapter 1 verse 7 in your Bible and learn it!

18 APRIL

Gold is a very special colour, isn't it? Gold is used very carefully because it is a very expensive material. Gold itself is actually a metal. It is a rare metal and is very precious. When we give someone something that is made of real gold it is a sign that we think very highly of them. Gold transforms things. That means it changes things so much you would not believe they were the same old thing! The Hebrew people in the Old Testament used gold much more than we do today because there was much more of it around! One of the things which the Hebrews made for their tabernacle or place of worship was a beautiful golden candlestick. This candlestick held seven candles. The "golden candlestick" are 2 words that don't seem to match. When you think of the word golden it suggests something valuable and ornate. But when you think of the word candlestick you think of a plain stick or a piece of wood which has been shaped to hold a candle. When the plain ordinary wood of a candlestick is replaced with gold - my oh my! It is something very special indeed. The beautiful gold of God's love, when it replaces our sinful nature makes us quite different people! The colour gold reminds us of the rich love of God.

> Can you think of something gold and how valuable it is?

19 APRIL

Silver is another unusual colour. But silver is much more common than gold and it is not as valuable. Silver is the colour of which most coins are made. The 30 coins for which Judas sold Jesus were silver in colour. We know this because in the book of Matthew, chapter 26 and verse 15 it tells us that Judas agreed to sell Jesus for "30 pieces of silver". When we see the silver of our coins we should remember that for very little indeed Judas betrayed his friend Jesus.

> **Judas betrayed Jesus for _ _ pieces of _ _ _ _ _ _**

20 APRIL

We all have colours which we like and colours which we don't like! When we choose clothes their colours are very important to us. A colour can make you really like something or a colour can make you really dislike something! We need to wear colours which suit us. Maybe you don't suit the colour green or maybe you really suit the colour brown. Your Mum or Dad help you choose colours which suit you.

There are things a bit like colours which suit us and don't suit us. These things are called manners. Manners describe how we behave - whether we behave rudely or pleasantly. For example, if we eat with our mouths open we are being bad mannered. If we say thank you when we are given something we are good mannered.

Bad manners don't suit anybody. Good manners are like bright colours and suit everybody. God considers our manners to be very important, so much so that He put a whole book on manners into the Bible. This book is called the book of Proverbs. It is in the Old Testament and is full of instructions. Things which we can do and things which we must not do - so that we are well mannered children of God.

> **Can you fill in the blanks in this sentence?**
>
> **Good manners are like bright c _ _ _ _ _ _ and s _ _ _ everyone**

21 APRIL

There was a man, a young man, in the Bible who was given a special coat of many colours. This young man was called Joseph and his Father gave him this beautiful coloured coat because he loved him very much.

Joseph's brothers were jealous that he had been given such a beautiful coat to wear and they took Joseph and put him in a pit. Then they took his lovely coat and put the blood of an animal over it and pretended to their Father that a wild animal must have killed Joseph!

What a rotten thing to do to their brother and all because he had been given a colourful coat!

Jealousy makes us spiteful. Spiteful people do very wicked things. It is better not to be jealous of other people because you only hurt yourself.

The story of Joseph is in the first book of the Bible, Genesis, chapter 37.

Jealously makes us

S _ _ _ _ _ _ _

Joseph had a lovely coat of many C _ _ _ _ _ _

22 APRIL

Some colours are very hard to find and to make. One such colour is the colour purple. The colour originates in a shellfish! The purple colour was found in a small vein of the fish and the rest of the fish was useless. Because purple was such a rare and costly colour to find, only the clothes of kings and queens were coloured purple. Another way to obtain the colour purple was from an insect which lived on a special kind of oak tree called the kermes oak. This colour purple was a bit like the colour we know as crimson or scarlet.

When Jesus was taken prisoner, before He was crucified, the Roman soldiers mocked Him and put a purple robe on Him. By doing this they were dressing Him up to look like a king. They put a crown made of thorns on His head which cut Him and caused Him to suffer great pain. The colour purple is a kingly colour.

Do you know the answers?

Purple was first found in

S _ _ _ _ F _ _ _ and

in an I _ _ _ _ _

23 APRIL

There is a story in the book of Acts chapter 16 about a lady named Lydia who sold the colour purple. Lydia was a good and kind woman. When Lydia heard about Jesus she accepted Him as her Lord and she showed kindness to Paul who had told her about Jesus.

Why don't you find the story of Lydia and the colour purple in your Bible and read it.

24 APRIL

Let's see what you can remember about some of the colours which we read about in the Bible.

★ The middle colour of the rainbow is B _ _ _.

★ Heaven above is the colour B _ _ _.

★ The sea reflects the colour B _ _ _ _.

★ The colour G _ _ _ _ reminds us of growth.

★ Our sins are the colour of a big B _ _ _ _ x.

★ The colour R _ _ reminds us of the blood of J _ _ _ _ _ which cleanses us from all sin.

★ When Jesus cleanses us we are made as W _ _ _ _ as snow.

★ The colour G _ _ _ transforms things and makes them very valuable.

★ Manners are like bright C _ _ _ _ _ _ _ which suit everyone.

★ Joseph had a coat of many C _ _ _ _ R _.

★ The colour P _ _ _ _ _ is a kingly colour.

★ There are ☐ colours in the rainbow.

25 APRIL

Some stories in the Bible have both colours and numbers in them. When Moses and Aaron were leading the children of Israel to their promised new land of Cannan they made a place of worship called the Tabernacle. God told Moses and Aaron to do this and because they were travelling it was made out of the same things as tents are made from. This meant that it could be carried with them. However this was a very elaborate tent and it was a special place for God to dwell so that He could always be close to them. All the details about the Tabernacle are contained in the book of Exodus. God's plan for the Tabernacle included colours and it used numbers to make it accurate.

The Tabernacle was the place were G _ _ dwelt.

26 APRIL

There were four materials used in the making of the Tabernacle. These were:

1. GOLD
2. SILVER
3. BRASS
4. WOOD

And there were 4 types of covering used over the Tabernacle. These were:

1. GOAT'S HAIRS
2. RAM'S SKINS
3. BADGER SKINS
4. FINE LINEN

So you see that the number 4 is an important number in the story of the Tabernacle.

How many materials were used to make the Tabernacle?

F _ _ _

How many coverings were used over the Tabernacle?

F _ _ _

27 APRIL

The colours of the Tabernacle were beautiful. These colours were used in the curtains which divided different areas of the Tabernacle from one another. The four colours of the curtains were

1. **BLUE**
2. **PURPLE**
3. **SCARLET**
4. **PATTERNED WITH CHERUBIMS**

These colours made the tabernacle a very attractive and lovely place.

Can you draw pictures of what you think the four curtains of the Tabernacle were like?

BLUE

PURPLE

SCARLET

CHERUBIM

28 APRIL

The story about the making of the Tabernacle teaches us that it is important that we have a special place where we can go to worship God. We call this place of worship our Church. We can take friends to Church with us so that they will learn about God's love for them. This is called the Gospel. God requires that our Ministers preach the gospel faithfully. That means that they must tell the people who come into their church the truth of the Word of God so that they will learn that Jesus died for their sins.

Can you fill in the blanks?

The G _ _ _ _ _ lets people know that Jesus dies for their S _ _ _

29 APRIL

When God got the children of Israel to set up the Tabernacle He told them that it was to be kept in good order because it was the place where He dwelt.
Our bodies are a bit like the Tabernacle. God requires that we keep ourselves clean and tidy because we are His children.
We should take pleasure in keeping ourselves clean and tidy. We should clean our teeth and brush our hair. We should wash our dirty hands and bath ourselves so that all of our bodies are clean.
When Jesus returned to Heaven he left a special person to be with us. That person is called the Holy Spirit. He dwells in us. Our bodies are His Tabernacle.

What is the special person called who Jesus left with us?

He is called the H _ _ _   S _ _ _ _ _

30 APRIL

The month of April ends today. We have learnt about some numbers and some colours which are in the Bible. Of course there are many, many more stories about colours and numbers than these. Perhaps you can look for these yourself.

To finish this month why don't you draw a lovely picture of a rainbow and remember it has 7 colours!

1 MAY

Do you know what a miracle is? A miracle is something marvellous. It is something supernatural. A miracle is something that does not happen naturally. There are things which happen naturally which we can see happening every day and which we do every day. When we are tired we go to sleep - that is a natural thing to do. When we are happy we laugh - that is a natural thing to do. When we are hungry we eat - that is a natural thing to do. Sometimes we have to fight against natural things! If somebody is nasty to us we want to be nasty back! That is a natural reaction but it is not the best thing to do. It is better to ignore them and not be nasty like them.

A miracle is not a natural thing and when Jesus was on Earth He performed miracles to show to people that God was His Heavenly Father.

A miracle is a S _ P _ _ N _ T _ R _ L thing

2 MAY

Some of the miracles which Jesus did, He did on the Sabbath day. God created the Sabbath day as a day of rest and as a day when we can enjoy all the things God has given us in life - without having to work as well! It is nice to have a day without work, isn't it? Of course there are jobs that have to be done on Sunday. If someone is sick they have to be looked after - hospitals don't just close down on Sundays and we have necessary things to do on Sundays as well. We still wash ourselves and clean our teeth and help wash the dishes. These things are just things that have to be attended to. Jesus showed us that even on the Sabbath there were still things that it was proper to do. Some people didn't agree with this but if they were sick they would be mighty glad of help, even it if was Sunday! The important thing about Sunday is that we should enjoy it and make it a special day when we take time to think about God and thank Him for all the things He has done for us.

We should always
E
_
_
_
_
Sunday!

3 MAY

The first four books of the New Testament are

M _ _ _ H _ _
M _ R _
L _ _ E
J _ H _

When you read your Bible always look for things about
J _ _ _ _

In the books of the Bible called Matthew, Mark, Luke and John we have a record of Jesus' life on Earth. Of course not every single thing Jesus did is written down in these four books but some very interesting things are. Matthew, Mark, Luke and John are the first four books of the New Testament. These four men were disciples of Jesus. Other books in the Bible tell us things about Jesus as well.

When you read your Bible, above all else you should look for things about Jesus as you read it.

4 MAY

In the book of Matthew we learn about a man who had a very sore hand. In fact it was so sore that Matthew tells us it was withered. When something is withered it is dead. Perhaps you have seen a flower that has withered. It is all droopy and dry and the colour no longer is bright and fresh. If you touched it the petals would fall off.

Can you imagine how sore it would be to have a hand that was withered? Not only would it not look very nice - but you would not be able to use it.

When Jesus saw this man whose hand was of no use to him, He said to the man "stretch forth thine hand". And when the man did this his hand was restored! It was made just like his other hand! All healthy and useful - all nice looking again! Now that's a MIRACLE. Could you pick up a withered flower and make it grow again? Could you take an apple after it had gone rotten and make it firm and crisp and ready to be eaten? Of course not! Yet Jesus healed this man's hand by just telling him to stretch it out!

The miracle which Jesus did for the man with the withered hand is told to us by

M _ _ _ T _ W

This story is found in chapter 12 of his book.

5 MAY

When Jesus did the miracle for the man with the withered hand He didn't just do it to help the man. He did it to show to others the power of God, His Heavenly Father. Jesus met this man on a Sunday and some people who were around Him thought that because it **was** Sunday Jesus shouldn't help him. In fact these people were pretty sneaky because they actually asked Jesus if it was lawful for Him to heal on Sundays!

Imagine if you had a broken leg and there was a doctor nearby who could help you and at the same time there were people whose legs were perfectly all right standing around you. Imagine if one of those people said to the doctor - "Do you think you should help that person with the broken leg, after all it is Sunday!" Huh! It's all right for them - standing there with two perfectly healthy legs saying that, isn't it! You'd probably feel like breaking their legs too!! And the doctor wouldn't care what day of the week it was, if he could help you he would. But Jesus had a good answer for them!

> To find what Jesus said to the sneaky people look up Matthew chapter 12 verses 11 and 12, in your Bible.

6 MAY

The sneaky people who followed Jesus around and tried to find fault with Him were called Pharisees. Maybe you know someone who is like a Pharisee - always finding faults in other people and always acting better than other people. The word which you probably would use for a person like that is the word snob! Wouldn't you hate to be thought of as a snob! Jesus was very patient with these Pharisees. It sure is hard to be patient with people who are always trying to catch us out and who are always judging us! Jesus said that we should not make it our job to judge others but that we should spend all our time making sure we are doing what is pleasing to Him. You know the Pharisees were a miserable bunch! If they had followed Jesus they could have enjoyed His company and they would have been glad to see the man with the withered hand healed. Instead they went out and complained about it! What a bunch of stinkers they were!!

Jesus tells us not to J _ _ G _ others

7 MAY

Can you fill in the gaps in these questions?

★ The M _ R _ C _ E of the man with the withered hand can be read in the book of M _ TT _ _ W.

★ J _ _ _ _ healed the man's sore hand by saying 'S _ _ _ _ _ _ forth thine H _ _ _'.

★ Jesus performed this M _ R _ C _ E on the S _ _ _ _ _ _ day.

★ The P _ _ R _ S _ _ S did not think J _ _ _ _ should have helped the man on the Sabbath.

8 MAY

Mark also tells us in his book of MIRACLES which Jesus did on the Sabbath day. In the first chapter of Mark we are told about two MIRACLES Jesus did one Sabbath day.

Jesus was in the city of Capernaum and He had gone into the synagogue there and was teaching the people wonderful things about His Heavenly Father.

In the synagogue there was a man who had an unclean spirit. This unclean spirit lived inside this man and it did not like Jesus one little bit. So much so that it made the man shout at Jesus!

The unclean spirit was an angry wee brat and the unclean spirit was afraid of the power of God. Do you know why it was angry and afraid? It was angry and afraid because it knew that Jesus could destroy it. And that is exactly what Jesus did!

The MIRACLE of the unclean spirit can be read in the book of M _ _ _ chapter 1.

9 MAY

Jesus was stronger than the U _ _ _ _ _ _ spirit.

When Jesus heard the man who had the unclean spirit shouting at Him, He was not afraid because He knew that He could rid the man of this foul thing. Mark tells us that Jesus told the unclean spirit to come out of the man.

Now that dirty wee spirit put up a fight - but it was useless because Jesus was stronger and it had to obey Him and the man was freed from its control.

This MIRACLE amazed all the people who were in the synagogue and they told all their friends and neighbours what Jesus had done!

10 MAY

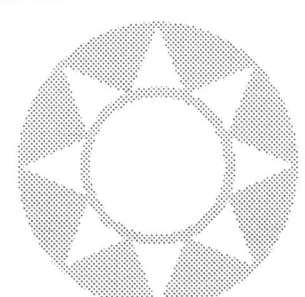

The same Sabbath day that Jesus performed the MIRACLE of destroying the unclean spirit, He went to the house of Simon and Andrew. Simon was married and his wife's mother was sick. Mark tells us that she had a fever. When Jesus heard that she was sick He went to see her and He took her hand and lifted her up. When Jesus did this she was made completely better! And she was made so better that she was able to tell what Jesus had done for her! That evening everyone in the city of Capernaum came to the doorway of Simon and Andrew's house and Jesus healed many people who were sick and cast out many devils from people.

Why don't you find Mark chapter one in your Bible and read about these MIRACLES.

11 MAY

Mark chapter one tells us about two MIRACLES which Jesus did on the Sabbath.
Can you remember something about them?
Let's see...

> ★ When Jesus was in the city of C _ _ E R _ _U M He performed the M_ _ A _ _ _ of the U _ _ _ _ _ _ spirit and He performed the Miracle of healing S_M _ N'S wife's mother who was sick with a F _ V _ _ .
>
> ★ All the people of the city of Capernaum came to Simon and A _ _ _ E W'S house that evening.
>
> ★ J _ _ _ _ healed many who were S _ _ _ and cast out many D _ V _ _ S .

12 MAY

In the book of Luke there are more examples of MIRACLES which Jesus did on the Sabbath day. Can you bend over and touch your toes? Just imagine if one day when you bent down to touch your toes or bent down to pick something up off the floor and your back stuck! You wouldn't be able to stand up straight. You wouldn't be able to see where you were going. You wouldn't be able to lie down flat and can you imagine how hard it would be to sit or dress or eat? Well, one Sabbath when Jesus was teaching He saw a woman who was bent over like that and He called her to come to Him. He put his hands on her and at once she was made straight. When He did this she thanked God for the MIRACLE which Jesus had performed. This woman had been bent over for 18 years! Wasn't it wonderful that He was able to heal her!

> Jesus made the bent woman's back
>
> ST_ _ _ _ HT

13 MAY

If you had seen Jesus heal the woman whose back was bent I'm sure you would have been very happy that she had been made better. But remember those Pharisees who complained about Jesus healing the man whose hand had withered? Well, sure enough there was another one of them around on the Sabbath day when Jesus healed that woman. Boy did he complain and told Jesus that He shouldn't do things like that on the Sabbath! This time Jesus told him what he was. He told him he was a HYPOCRITE! A hypocrite is a person who criticizes somebody for doing something which they do themselves! If your friend rode their bike across the garden and then you rode your bike across the garden and if they turned round and said to you "you shouldn't do that" - what would you say to them? You would say "sure you just did the same thing yourself!" That person would be a hypocrite for scolding you for doing the very thing which they did! So a hypocrite has double standards - one for you and one for themselves.

A hypocrite has
D
—
—
—
—
Standards

14 MAY

Jesus has no time for hypocrites! Luke tells us that when the man complained to Jesus for healing the woman with the bent back He pointed out to that man that he did things on the Sabbath day too! He used an example of what other people did to prove His point. The story about the MIRACLE of the woman being healed is in chapter 12 of the book of Luke. It commences at verse 10.

Why don't you find this story and read it and see what example Jesus gave to the man who complained. (Here is a clue - it is in verse 15.)

15 MAY

In the next chapter of the book of Luke, that is chapter 14, Jesus again performed a MIRACLE on the Sabbath day. This time Jesus was having something to eat. He was in one of the Pharisee's houses and the Pharisee whose house He was in, and the other Pharisees who were there too, watched Jesus. Don't you hate people who watch you, waiting for you to make a mistake so that they can yap at you! Well these Pharisees were watching Jesus so as they could complain again to Him.

Jesus knew that these Pharisees were just waiting for Him to do something which would give them an excuse to find fault.

Also in the house was a man who had a disease called dropsy. Jesus decided to ask these Pharisees a question!

> **Can you find the question Jesus asked the Pharisees?**
>
> **It is in Luke chapter 14 and verse 5.**

16 MAY

Jesus healed the man with the dropsy disease on a Sabbath day in the house of one of the Pharisees. Before He healed him He asked the Pharisees a question. Did you find the question? He asked them if one of their animals fell into a pit on the Sabbath day would they help it out? Do you know what the Pharisees answer was to that? What do you think they said. If you had a dog and it fell down a hole on a Sunday would you wait until Monday to rescue it? Of course not! You would help it straight away.

When Jesus asked the Pharisees this simple question they knew that they would rescue their animals on a Sunday but before they would admit it, they said nothing! Nothing at all! They didn't answer the question which Jesus asked them because they were hypocrites!

So Jesus took the poor diseased man and lovingly made him better from his terrible disease. This time the Pharisees couldn't complain!

> **What was the answer which the Pharisees gave to Jesus' question?**
>
> **N _ T _ _ _ G!**

17 MAY

Luke tells us about two MIRACLES which Jesus did on the Sabbath day. Can you fill in the spaces and see how much you can remember about these MIRACLES?

- The W _ _ _ _ who Jesus healed had a B _ _ _ back. Her B _ _ _ was B _ _ _ _ for _ _ years! When Jesus healed her she gave thanks to G _ _.

- Jesus healed the man from the disease called D _ _ _ _ _ _.

- The Pharisees did not like J _ _ _ _ _ doing M _ _ _ _ _ _ _ _ on the S _ BB _ _ H.

- These M _ _ _ _ _ _ _ _ are found in the book of L _ _ _ chapters _ and _ _.

18 MAY

Matthew, Mark and Luke all tell us about MIRACLES which Jesus did on the Sabbath day. John also tells us about two MIRACLES which Jesus did on the Sabbath. One Sabbath day, Jesus was in Jerusalem and He was at the pool of Bethesda. This pool had five porches and in these porches lay a whole lot of people who were impotent. Impotent means they had some part of their body which did not work properly. John tells us some had eyes which were blind. Some had legs which could not walk. Some had hands that were withered. These poor, sick people all lay waiting for the water in the pool of Bethesda to move because when it moved the first who stepped into the pool were healed.

The pool of B _ _ _ _ _ _ _ had F _ _ _ porches

19 MAY

When Jesus saw a certain man who was sick lying beside the pool He asked him if he wanted to be made better. This man, who had been unable to walk for 38 years, told Jesus that he had no one to help him into the pool. Jesus just said to him "rise, take up thy bed and walk". And that man immediately was able to stand up and walk!

> **What did Jesus say to the man?**
> "Rise, take up thy **B** _ _ and walk."

20 MAY

The second MIRACLE which John tells us about that Jesus performed on the Sabbath can be read in chapter 9 of his book. It is the story of how Jesus healed the eyes of a man who was born blind. To perform this MIRACLE, Jesus spat on the ground and made clay of the spittle. He then spread the clay upon the eyes of the blind man. Then Jesus told him to go and wash in the pool of Siloam. When the man did this he came back and he could see! Once again the fact that Jesus performed a MIRACLE on the Sabbath meant that the Pharisees gave off! But on this occasion they started to fight with themselves too!

> If you want to read about the row the Pharisees had find the book of John chapter 9 and it tells you all about it!

21 MAY

Matthew, Mark, Luke and John all tell us about miracles which Jesus did on the Sabbath day. There are seven miracles which are in the Bible which Jesus performed on the Sabbath. These are the seven Sabbath miracles. Let's see if you can remember some things about them.

★ M _ _ _ _ _ W tells us about the M _ _ _ _ _ _ _ of the withered H _ _ _.

★ M _ _ _ tells us about the M _ _ _ _ _ _ S of the unclean S _ _ R _ _ and of Simon's wife's mother being healed of her F _ V _ _.

★ L _ _ _ tells us about the M _ _ _ _ _ _ S of the woman with the bent B _ _ _ _ and the man with the disease called D _ _ P _ _.

★ J _ _ _ tells us about the M _ _ _ _ _ _ _ S of the man who couldn't W _ _ K and the man who was born B _ _ N _.

22 MAY

We have just been reading about seven MIRACLES which Jesus did on the Sabbath day. Of course Jesus performed many other MIRACLES some of which are in the books of Matthew, Mark, Luke and John. When you are reading these books you should see how many other MIRACLES Jesus did that you can find.

There are more than 30 MIRACLES written about for us to read! To help you find these over the next few days we will look for them together!

23 MAY

Let's find these three MIRACLES in our Bibles today!

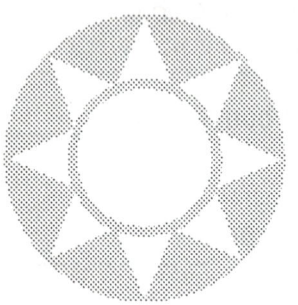

1. The MIRACLE of the water turned into wine.
   John chapter 2 verse 1-11.
2. The MIRACLE of the nobleman's son cured.
   John chapter 5 verses 46-54
3. The MIRACLE of the fishes.
   Luke chapter 5 verses 1-11.

24 MAY

Yesterday you found three MIRACLES in your Bible - shall we find three more today?

These are easy and they are all in the book of Mark and one of them you already know!

1. Look up **Mark chapter 1 verses 23-26** and you will find the MIRACLE of how the man who had demons in him was cured!
2. Stay in the same chapter of **Mark** and in **verses 31 and 32** you will find a MIRACLE that we have already learned about!
3. Read on further down the chapter and at **verse 40 through to 45** you will find the MIRACLE of the leper cleansed. Isn't this first chapter of the book of Mark full of MIRACLES!

Did you remember the MIRACLE about Simon's wife's mother?

25 MAY

I think you could find four MIRACLES today. To make it fun we will look for one in the book of Luke and three in the book of Matthew.

The three MIRACLES to look for in Matthew today can be found in **Matthew chapter 8**.

One is in **verses 5-13** and it is the MIRACLE of the centurion's servant being healed.

Two is in **verses 23-27** and it is the MIRACLE of the tempest being calmed.

Three is in **verses 28-34** and it is the MIRACLE of the Demonlacs of Gadara being cured.

The one MIRACLE to look for in Luke today is a very special one because it is the MIRACLE of the widow's son being raised from the dead! It is in **Luke chapter 7 verses 11-17**.

26 MAY

Here are just two MIRACLES to find today seeing as you worked so hard yesterday!

They are both in the book of Matthew.

1. **Matthew chapter 9 verses 1-8** the MIRACLE of the man sick of the palsy cured.
2. In the same chapter if you look down to **verse 18** you will find the MIRACLE of Jairus' daughter.

Now, wasn't that easy?

27 MAY

Now yesterday was an easy day! You only had two MIRACLES to find. Today we will look for four - but one of them you already know! We will use three books of the Bible today to find these MIRACLES.

1. **Matthew chapter 10 verse 27-31**. The MIRACLE of the blind men.
2. **Matthew chapter10 verses 32 and 31**. The MIRACLE of the dumb man.
3. **Luke chapter 8 verses 43-48**. The MIRACLE of the woman diseased with an issue of blood.
and
4. This one you know already. Can you remember it? The MIRACLE of the man at the pool of Bethesda. It is in **John chapter 5 verses 1-9**.

> Were you able to find all of these MIRACLES?

28 MAY

Because you worked hard yesterday and found four miracles, today we will find just two MIRACLES which we haven't read about yet and two MIRACLES which you already know.

The two which you know are in **Matthew chapter12**. The MIRACLE of the withered hand **(verses 10-13)** and the MIRACLE of the man with the unclean spirit **(verses 22-23)**. The two new ones are also in the book of **Matthew.** The first is in **chapter 14** and it is the MIRACLE of the five thousand being fed. The second is in **chapter 15** and it is the MIRACLE of the Canaanite woman's daughter being healed.

> Which story of these MIRACLES do you like best?

29 MAY

o you know that already you have found 20 MIRACLES in your Bible.
Today we will find 2 MIRACLES in the book of Matthew and 2 MIRACLES in the book of Mark.

The two in Matthew are:

1. **Chapter 15 verses 32-39**. The miracle of the four thousand fed.
2. **Chapter 17 verses 14-21**. The miracle of the boy who was possessed of a devil being healed.

The two in Mark are

1. **Chapter 7 verses 31-37**. The miracle of the man who was deaf and dumb being healed.
2. **Chapter 8 verses 22-26**. The miracle of the blind man being given his sight.

Did you find all four?

30 MAY

Today we are going to find five MIRACLES but this will be very easy because you already know three of them.
So you are only finding two new ones.

The first two to find are in the book of John and they are both in chapter 9.
One of these you know about already - it is the MIRACLE of the man who was born blind being healed. The new one is the MIRACLE of Lazarus being raised from the grave.
The next three MIRACLES to find are in the book of Luke - but you know two of these already.
The two you know are the MIRACLE of the woman with the bent back - chapter 13 verses 11-17 and the MIRACLE of the man with the disease called dropsy - chapter 14 verses 11-4.
The new one to find is the miracle of the 10 lepers being cleansed. It is in chapter 17 verses 11-19.

Today you have found five MIRACLES! and you already knew three of these MIRACLES and you found two new ones - Well done!

31 MAY

There are just four MIRACLES left for you to find in your Bible.

Two are in Matthew.
One is in Luke.
And one is in John
See how quickly you can find these last four MIRACLES!

1. **Matthew chapter 20 vs 30-31**. The MIRACLE of two blind men healed.
2. **Matthew chapter 21 verses 18-21**. The MIRACLE of the fig tree cursed.
3. **Luke chapter 22 verses 50 and 51**. The MIRACLE of the ear being healed.
4. **John chapter 21 verses 1-14**. The MIRACLE of the draught of fishes.

You have found in you Bible thirty miracles! All these miracles teach us many things. We don't learn all these things at once so each time you hear about or read about Jesus and His miracles think carefully about the things which they teach you.

1 JUNE

When God created the world He did not just create the trees and plants so that the world looked nicer. He created them also because they have a job to do.

Trees and plants provide us with fruit and flowers and they keep the air fresh and clean for us to breathe.

Trees and plants are necessary for animals. Many animals live in trees and they need the leaves and the fruit of the trees, and the grass of the field for food.

God uses trees and plants and animals to teach us many things.

The first tree from which God teaches us something very important is the unique tree which was planted in the centre of the garden in Eden.

> **Can you remember the name of the unique tree?**
>
> The tree of KN _ _ L _ D _ E of good and E _ _ L

2 JUNE

The tree of knowledge of good and evil teaches us about **DISOBEDIENCE**. It teaches us that when we DISOBEY, things change. Adam and Eve disobeyed God's rule about the unique tree. They did the very thing that God told them not to do! Because of this everything changed!

> **When we disobey things**
>
> C _ _ _ _ _

3 JUNE

The first thing that changed when Adam and Eve disobeyed God was that they knew they had done wrong. When you do something which you have been told not to do, you know fine well that you have disobeyed, don't you! Adam and Eve knew for the first time that they were naked and they tried to cover themselves by taking leaves from another tree - the fig tree - and making aprons out of those leaves.

Sometimes when we do what is wrong we try to hide what we have done. But that is a useless thing to do because it doesn't undo our wrong.

> **What kind of a tree did Adam and Eve take the leaves from to make their aprons?**
>
> A F _ _ Tree

4 JUNE

Imagine thinking that clothes made from leaves would last! Adam and Eve didn't think very well when they did such a silly thing to try and cover themselves. We are often like Adam and Eve and do some daft things to try and cover our own wrong doing. The next thing which changed when Adam and Eve disobeyed was their friendship with God. For the first time Adam and Eve hid from God!

Do you ever hide yourself away when you have done something bad? Why do you do that? You do that because you know somebody is going to be cross with you! You are ashamed of what you have done. Do you know where Adam and Eve hid? They hid among the trees.

> **Adam and Eve hid from God because they were**
>
> A _ _ _ _ _ _ _

5 JUNE

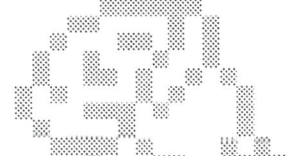

Even the trees could not stop God from looking for Adam and Eve. God called Adam. When He spoke to him He asked him if he had eaten of the unique tree. Now everything changed. Adam and Eve could no longer stay in the Garden of Eden. The beautiful serpent who had lied to Eve was made into a cursed beast that could only slide around on its belly. And even the Earth was changed because for the first time plants would have thorns and thistles. My, how different things became for Adam and Eve when they disobeyed God!

What did plants start to have after Adam and Eve disobeyed God?

TH _ _ _ S and TH _ _ _ _ _ S

6 JUNE

Something else very sad also happened when Adam and Eve sinned. The leaves of the fig tree were useless as clothes for them. They wouldn't last long and they wouldn't protect them. So God had to make them coats of skins to clothe them. That meant that God had to take the skins of animals to cover Adam and Eve. If Adam and Eve had not disobeyed, God would not have had to kill these animals to cover them. The poor animals which died had not been bad yet they had to be hurt because of what Adam and Eve did. When we do what is wrong it hurts other people.

What did God make Adam and Eve?

C _ _ _ _

of

S _ _ _ _

7 JUNE

The trees and the animals in the Garden of Eden teach us some very, very important things.

We learn that when we disobey, things change.
We learn that hiding doesn't change the fact that we have done what is wrong.
We learn that when we do what is wrong other people get hurt.
We also learn that God didn't just put Adam and Eve out of the Garden set in Eden without giving them coats first to cover them. God has given us a special covering for our wrong doing as well. That covering is the precious blood of Jesus Christ, His Son.

Can you fill in the missing letters?

God made C _ _ _ S for Adam

and Eve and God has made a special

C _ V _ _ I _ G for us

8 JUNE

The most special tree in the Bible is the tree which became the cross on which Jesus died to take away the big black **X** of our wrong doing. On that tree Jesus shed His precious blood so that our sins are completely taken away from us.

Just as the animals in the Garden of Eden had not done anything wrong yet they had to die to provide coats for Adam and Eve. So too, Jesus had not done anything wrong yet He had to die on the tree which became His cross to provide a cover for our sins. Jesus loved us very, very deeply to do such a thing for us.

The most special tree in the Bible is the

C
_
_
_
_
on which Jesus died

9 JUNE

The thorns which had grown on the Earth because of Adam and Eve's sin were used by the Roman soldiers to make a crown of thorns to put on Jesus' head. This crown pierced into His skin and hurt Jesus very badly and caused Him to bleed. Our sins are just like those thorns and thistles. They are sharp and prickly and cause us pain. Jesus heals the pain and sorrow of our sins and where we were cut by them He makes us whole again.

This is the greatest MIRACLE of all MIRACLES.
It is our salvation!

> **Jesus had a crown made of**
>
> T _ _ _ _ _ put on His head

10 JUNE

In the book of Genesis chapter 22 we here are told about a man and his son and an animal. The man was called Abraham. His son was called Isaac. The animal was a ram.

One day God said to Abraham that He wanted him to offer his son Isaac as a sacrifice to Him. Abraham was a friend of God and he knew that God would not ask him to do anything without a purpose. Even though Abraham did not know God's reason for asking him to do such a thing, Abraham obeyed God.

He took Isaac, his son, and went to the land of Moriah where God showed him the place where he was to make his sacrifice.

Can you imagine how the man Abraham must have felt, knowing that he was going to have to sacrifice his own son!

Isn't that what God did for you and me?

He sent His own Son, Jesus Christ, to die on the cross for us!

> A
> B
> _
> _ H
> _
> M
> **obeyed God**

11 JUNE

Abraham and Isaac climbed together to the place that God had showed Abraham. Abraham built an altar and took his son whom he loved very dearly and bound him and laid him on the altar and was ready to use his knife to slay him, when the Angel of the Lord called out to him from Heaven and told him not to do his son any harm, because his obedience had proved that his friendship to God was true. And there was a ram caught in a thicket which Abraham had to use for his sacrifice.

This story of the man Abraham, his son Isaac and the ram shows us that when we obey God we are rewarded and not punished the way Adam and Eve had to be when they disobeyed God.

Do you think you can draw a picture of a ram - it is just like a sheep with horns!

12 JUNE

Let's see how much you can remember about the animals and trees.

★ What was the name of the unique tree that Adam and Eve ate from?
The tree of knowledge of G _ _ D and E _ _ L.

★ What kind of tree did Adam and Eve make their aprons from?
A F _ _ tree.

★ What kind of coats did God make for Adam and Eve?
Coats of S _ _ _ _ .

★ What happened to the serpent?
It was made go everywhere on its B _ _ _ _ .

★ What is the most special tree that we learn about in the Bible?
The tree which became the C _ _ _ _ .

★ What started to grow among the plants when Adam and Eve disobeyed God?
T _ _ _ S and T _ _ _ _ _ _ S.

★ What did the soldiers put on the head of Jesus?
A C _ _ W _ of T _ _ _ N _ .

★ What was the name of the man who was God's friend?
A B _ _ H _ M.

★ His son Isaac was replaced on the altar by what animal?
A R _ _ .

13 JUNE

If you find the book of Jonah and find chapter 1 and verse 2 you will read there what God wanted Jonah to do.

You have probably heard about a man called Jonah and how he was swallowed by a great fish!

There is a book in the Bible called the book of Jonah, which tells us lots of things about this man. The book of Jonah is in the Old Testament and it has just 4 chapters.

The reason why Jonah wound up in the belly of a great big fish was because he was running away from doing a job that God asked him to do.

14 JUNE

God wanted Jonah to go to a city called Nineveh and tell the people of that city that they needed to obey God. Jonah couldn't be bothered doing this so he went and got a boat that was going to another place, went down inside the boat, found a nice comfy place to have a sleep and dozed off.

The next thing he knew was when the captain of the ship woke him up and told him he'd better start talking to his God because there was an awful storm and if it didn't stop blowing and raging so badly the boat was going to sink.

Jonah admitted to the other people on the boat that he was running away from a job God has asked him to do.

Then do you know what Jonah said to them? He said that they should throw him into the sea because his disobedience was the cause of the storm!

What did Jonah do when he got on to the boat?

He fell

A _ _ _ _ _ _ !

15 JUNE

You know, I think Jonah was crazy! If I was in a boat and there was an awful storm I can tell you there is no way that I'd want to be thrown into the sea, would you?! Well, God knew that Jonah would end up in the sea because when he told the others that they should throw him overboard that is exactly what they did! The sea calmed when this happened and the great fish which God had in the sea, swallowed Jonah!

Can you draw a picture of what you think the great fish looked like ?

16 JUNE

When Jonah was in the tummy of this great big fish he knew there was only one thing to do and that was to talk to God.

What did Jonah do when he was in the belly of the fish?

He T _ _ K _ _ to God

This pleased God because He knew Jonah had learned that his disobedience had caused the storm. It meant that instead of going to do the job God has asked of him, he wound up inside the great fish!
So God made the great fish sick!
And the fish vomited Jonah out of its belly on to dry land.

17 JUNE

God told Jonah for the second time to go to the city of Nineveh and to tell the people there about Him. This time Jonah did go to Nineveh. God told Jonah that he was to tell the people of this city that in 40 days the city would be overthrown, because the people were disobedient to God. The people, when they heard this from Jonah, believed him and were sorry for their wrong doing - even the king of Nineveh repented and ordered everyone in the city to ask God for mercy.

God heard their prayers and forgave them and decided that He would not destroy Nineveh.

Did Jonah obey God the second time? Tick the right box!

YES ☐

NO ☐

18 JUNE

The fact that God decided not to punish Nineveh didn't make Jonah one bit happy at all, and he went off in a sulk. In fact, he was so annoyed that he went out of the city and found another cozy place and sat there to see if God would punish the city after all. Jonah told God that he thought it would be better if he just died!

God allowed a plant called a gourd to grow beside Jonah to give him shadow for protection but God also made ready a hungry worm which ate the gourd the next morning!

God made a F _ _ _ which ate Jonah and

God made a W _ _ _ which ate the gourd.

19 JUNE

Now because the worm ate the gourd it meant that the sun shone straight down on top of Jonah's head! This hot sun made Jonah faint, and he still wished he would die. In fact Jonah had pity on the gourd because the worm had eaten it and made it die! God said to Jonah that if he had pity on a plant like the gourd which only lived for one night - how much more pity ought he to have on the city of Nineveh which had thousands of people and animals living in it!

Can you fill in the gaps in this sentence?

God had P _ _ _

on the people of

N _ N _ _ _ H.

20 JUNE

God used three things to teach Jonah to obey Him. Can you remember what they were? One was a plant and two were creatures. See if you can answer these questions.

★ The plant was called a G _ _ _ _ _.

★ The creatures were a great F _ _ _ and a W _ _ _ .

★ God made the F _ _ _ eat J _ _ _ _ _.

★ God made the W _ _ _ eat the G _ _ _ _ _.

★ Jonah had P _ _ _ on the gourd.

★ God had P _ _ _ on the people of N _ N _ _ _ H.

★ God F _ R _ _ _ E the people and the King when they were sorry.

21 JUNE

Here is a song about some birds called ravens which obeyed God

The ravens' wings went flap, flap, flap
As down to the river they flew.
They carried meat,
They carried bread,
As God had told them to.
A little widow woman
Was picking up sticks
As Elijah passed her way
She baked him a cake from oil and meal
That never would pass away!

The story about these ravens is found in the book of 1 Kings chapter 17. Why don't you find it in your Bible.

22 JUNE

Lions are about 8 feet long and about 4 feet high. That's pretty big isn't it? Added to this they are wild and ferocious animals. Oh, they are very lovely looking - they have a flowing mane, big shaggy eyebrows, and glittering teeth - but they could eat you alive! Samson was such a strong man that he killed one of these animals with his bare hands! Now that's strong! **In the book of Judges in chapter 14 you can read how Samson did this!**

Can you draw a picture of a lion?

23 JUNE

When Samson killed the lion a swarm of bees made their home in its carcass, and Samson saw this when he went back to look at the dead lion. Samson took this honey and ate some of it. He also gave some of this honey to two other people. Do you know who those people were?

The answer is found in Judges chapter 14 and verse 9. When you look this up fill in the gaps in this sentence.

The two other people which Samson gave honey from the lion were his M_ _ _ _ _ and his F_ _ _ _ _.

24 JUNE

David also killed a lion! In fact he killed a lion and a bear. Both of these animals are strong. I sure wouldn't want to try and see which was the stronger! This lion and this bear tried to steal one of the sheep which David was looking after. David chased the lion and the bear and rescued the sheep from the mouth of the lion and the bear!

If you find the book of 1 Samuel chapter 17 and look at verse 34 you will be able to read this story for yourself.

Can you draw a picture of a bear?

25 JUNE

Another man who came face to face with lions was Daniel. Daniel was actually thrown into a whole den of lions! Daniel did a very, very wise thing when this happened - he prayed. He asked God to close the lions' mouths so that they would not do him any harm. And God heard his prayer and the lions did Daniel no harm!
In the book of Daniel chapter 6 you will find this story - why don't you read it!

26 JUNE

There is a little tiny creature which God has created that He tells us we should look at and learn from.

This creature is the ant. Ants are very busy little things - they aren't slothful. God likes us to not be slothful. Do you know what slothful means? It means lazy and careless. There are lots of ways in which we can be careless, aren't there? We can be careless about how we dress. We can be careless about how we talk. We can be careless with the things we own. We can be careless with other people's things. God wants us to be careful people.

God wants us to be like the ant who is not

SL _ _ _ F _ _

27 JUNE

Another tiny creature that God talks about in the Bible is the little sparrow. God uses this little bird to explain how much He is concerned about us, and to tell us how He will always look after us. He says that even when one wee sparrow dies in the whole world, that He knows this and if He knows that about such a tiny creature, how much more does He know about you and me!

God sees even a little

SP _ _ _ _ W bird die.

28 JUNE

Throughout the Bible there are many stories which have all kinds of animals and trees and plants in them.
You have only read a few of them.
There are just two days left in this month.
On these two days there are two drawings. Beside these drawings why don't you write in just a few words what you remember about these animals.

103

29 JUNE

30 JUNE

1 JULY

Super Christian

Do you have a hero? I suppose before you answer that question you need to know what a hero is! A hero is not a wig! A hero is not a bike! A hero is not a bowl of cornflakes! Of course it is not!!
A hero is a champion! The Bible is full of champions - people whom we can admire.

What is a hero?

A hero is a _ _ A _ P _ _ _

2 JULY

When David slew the lion and the bear which tried to kill the sheep he was minding, he was very brave indeed. The little lamb which they took would have died if David had not rescued it.

Of course it is not a brave thing to kill any animal just for the sake of killing. That is not the act of a hero - that is the act of a coward. But if a wild animal is doing something wrong, sometimes it has to be killed. If David had let the bear and the lion go on taking the sheep - all the sheep would have died. Besides, the bear and the lion would, sooner or later, have killed David as well. David knew he had to face the danger of the lion and the bear if he was to protect the sheep. Heroes face danger.

Only cowards K _ _ _ animals for no purpose.

Heroes face D _ _ _ _ _

3 JULY

Usually when a person is brave once, they are able to be brave again. David was a hero again when he took Goliath on! If David had not fought the lion and the bear he would not have had the courage to fight a giant! If you do something that is right - even if it is a hard thing to do, you will find that it is easier to choose to do right the next time. After all, it is just as easy to do what is right as it is to do what is wrong!

> It is just as easy to do
>
> R _ _ _ _
>
> as it is to do
>
> W _ _ _ _

4 JULY

Heroes are champions, and the things that they do mean that we look up to them. But it is not fair to expect our heroes to be perfect people. They are only people like us, and they don't always do everything right. David became king of Israel and even though he was a hero and did many good and brave things - he also made mistakes! As you read your Bible you will learn about some of the mistakes he made. When David asked God to forgive him for his mistakes, God did. Perhaps the bravest thing David did was admitting that he had done what was wrong. It takes a good deal of courage to admit we are wrong.

> Heroes are only P _ _ _ _ _
> like us. They are not
>
> P
> _
> _
> _
> _
> _

5 JULY

Heroes are independent people. That means they are people who think for themselves. They don't listen to moaners like the Pharisees. They don't listen to the Devil. They don't listen to other people who would tell them to do wrong. They choose to listen to what God says and do their own thinking. If David had listened to the people who were all around him when he went to fight Goliath - he never would have fought him. He would have given up! If God didn't intend us to be independent people He would just have made us all the same. But God has made us with the ability to think for ourselves. Independence gives us freedom and God wants us to guard our freedom.

> Heroes are I _ _ _ P _ N _ _ _ T people.
>
> Independence give us F _ _ _ _ _ M.

6 JULY

Moses was quite a champion too. He was very brave when he went to Pharaoh and asked him to free the children of Egypt. Pharaoh was a powerful and cruel man but Moses met him face to face. You know, the best thing we can do when we are afraid is to be like Moses and face the things that we are afraid of. Heroes like Moses, don't pretend they are not frightened, they admit their fears, ask God to help them and then face their fears.

> Heroes like Moses face
>
> F _ _ _
>
> and ask
>
> G _ _
>
> to help them.

7 JULY

Like David, Moses too was not perfect. He was just an ordinary man. Remember what he did to the rock? He hit the rock instead of speaking to it, and God had to tell Moses that because of his disobedience he would not enter the promised land. Did Moses sulk with God and stop obeying Him? No, he did not. That made Moses a real champion. Because he took his punishment and continued to obey God.

Heroes take their

P _ N _ _ _ M _ _ T

8 JULY

Another time Moses showed how a hero behaves, was when the Children of Israel were being chased by Pharaoh. There was Moses leading thousands of people, and hot on their heels was Pharaoh and his crew! And what was Moses faced with - a sea! Did Moses flinch an inch? No. He trusted God and right up until the very second God divided the sea for the Children of Israel, Moses kept walking on. This behaviour isn't the behaviour of a Pharisee. This is the behaviour of a man who knew that God was right and that Pharaoh was wrong, and that the only thing to do was go on and not quit.

Super Christian

Moses didn't

F _ _ _ _ _

an

I
_
_
_

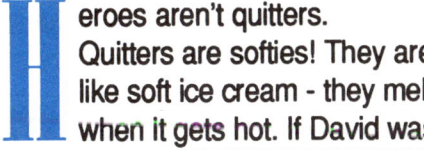

Heroes aren't quitters. Quitters are softies! They are like soft ice cream - they melt when it gets hot. If David was a quitter, he would have melted when he saw the size of the giant. If Moses was a quitter, he would have melted when he saw the size of the Red Sea. If Daniel was a quitter, he would have melted when he saw the size of the lions' mouths.

Heroes don't

Q _ _ _ !

If you don't quit it means you finish the job.
Champions finish the job - that ensures they are champions.

Moses didn't take the people halfway across the Red Sea and then stop! David didn't put the pebble into his sling, and then set the sling down on to the ground and walk away! Daniel didn't look at those lions' mouths and sit down and cry!
Oh no - Moses took the children the whole way across - David swung that sling and let the pebble whiz through the air and land right on target - and Daniel had more wit than to sit down and cry tears, he looked to God and cried for help.
These heroes finished the job. A person who leaves a job unfinished isn't even half a hero. Heroes finish the job.

Do you think you could draw a picture of David's sling in this space?

11 JULY

The jobs that champions do are always done properly. There is nothing worse than a job done wrongly. If you asked somebody to fix a puncture on your bike, and instead of them finding the hole in your tyre and patching it, they just pumped some air into it so that it looked fixed - you would be pretty mad, wouldn't you? You would think the job was done but when you tried to ride the bike you would soon know that the job wasn't done properly!

Remember: Heroes do a job properly!

David didn't just knock the giant Goliath out and then leave him. If he had done that, Goliath would have just wakened up again and come after David. David made sure Goliath was dead! There was no way he was going to just half kill him, so he cut his head off. A job half done is a job not done at all - because it has to be done all over again!

Super Christian

12 JULY

You don't have to be a man to be a champion. Champions come in all ages, shapes and sizes, and are both male and female.

Deborah and Jael were two women who were heroines. Do you know what they did? They got rid of a man called Sisera who was a captain in the army of king Jabin, the king of Canaan. This army was opposed to the Children of Israel and God used these two courageous women to slay him.

Jael actually hammered a nail through the head of Sisera. What a gory thing for anybody to do! But in battle some awful things happen. If Sisera had not been beaten in this war, hundreds of other people would have been slain by him.

The story of Deborah and Jael can be read in the book of Judges chapter 4

Heroes are not all M _ _ some Bible heroes are W _ _ _ _

13 JULY

Let's see how much you can remember about heroes!

- A hero is a C H _ _ P _ _ N.
- Heroes face D _ _ G _ R.
- Heroes do what is R _ G _ _.
- Heroes are not PER _ E _ T.
- Heroes are I N _ _ P _ _ D _ _ T.
- Heroes face their F _ A _ S and ask G _ _ to H _ _ P them.
- Heroes take their P _ N I S _ M E _ _ and still do what is right.
- Heroes don't FL _ N _ H an I N _ _ !
- Heroes aren't QU I _ _ _ RS!
- Heroes finish the J _ _.
- Heroes do the job P R O P _ _ _ Y.

14 JULY

There are people whom we learn about in history who are also heroes of our faith. Their names may not be in the Bible but they also can be admired by us. An example of one such hero is a man called Martin Luther. Martin Luther learned the meaning of a verse in the Bible which said "The just shall live by faith". This means that the children of God have eternal life because their faith, or their trust, is in God and not in anyone or anything else.

Can you learn Martin Luther's verse?

'The just shall live by faith'
(Romans 1 verse 17).

15 JULY

Do you remember when we were looking at numbers that remind us of things in the Bible?

What did the number one teach us? It taught us that God made one way to Heaven. Martin Luther had been told by the Church of Rome that there were many things that had to be done to get to Heaven. He had not learned that there was only one thing which could take away the big black ✘ of his sins and that was the blood of Jesus. He thought he had to do lots and lots of good things to take away that big black ✘ himself.

> Martin Luther learned that there was just O _ _ way to HE _ V _ _.

16 JULY

Martin Luther, when he read Romans chapter one, realised that all his works couldn't take away his sin. Martin Luther started to tell other people what he had learned, but the men in the Church of Rome were angry at him for disagreeing with them and there was a huge big row! Martin Luther had to defend what he believed.

Heroes defend their beliefs. That means they don't back down when their beliefs are challenged.

Super Christian

> Heroes, like Martin Luther, defend their
>
> B _ _ _ _ _ S

17 JULY

When Martin Luther defended his beliefs the whole world heard about it and the **'Reformation'** began.
The Reformation was the time in history when people abandoned or left the ideas of the Church of Rome and followed instead the leadership of Martin Luther.
Martin Luther began the Reformation.

Can you draw a picture of what you think Martin Luther looked like?

18 JULY

Martin Luther was not the only man who was involved with the Reformation, but he was the man who God chose to begin the changes which took place in the history of the church. This is the reason that we have the Protestant faith today.
Martin Luther was a champion because he had to stand alone and defend his beliefs.
Heroes are prepared to do what they believe is right even if they have to do it alone.

Heroes are prepared to do what is right even if they are

A _ _ _ E

19 JULY

It is much easier to do something which is hard if you have someone else with you.

Very often we have to be prepared to do what we know is right, all by ourselves.

Is God always with us? Tick the right box!

YES ☐

NO ☐

If we feel we are alone, we ought to remember that God is always near us to keep us company, and to help us to do the right thing.

A champion remembers that his ability comes from God, and when he has to do a job alone, he knows God is with him.

20 JULY

Just as we need the help of heroes, heroes need the help of other people in their lives as well.

Moses needed two people to help him during a battle. This battle can be read about in the book of Exodus chapter 17 and verse 11.

When Moses held up his hand, Israel succeeded in the battle, but when he let his hand down, Israel's enemy succeeded.

If you try and hold your hands up they soon get tired, don't they? Moses needed two people to hold his hands up for him. Aaron his brother held one of his hands up and Hur held up his other hand.

Heroes need the H _ _ _ of other P _ _ _ _ _

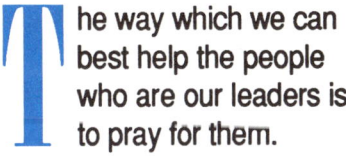
21 JULY

The way which we can best help the people who are our leaders is to pray for them.

You should pray for your minister because God has given him the job to teach people that they need Jesus. That is his job. Your job and the job of all the other people in your church is the job of praying that God will help your minister to be a hero of the faith.

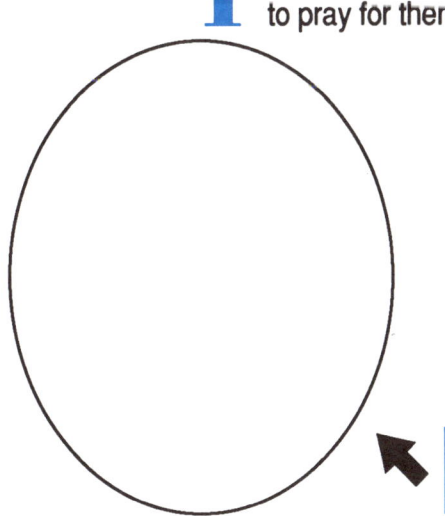

Can you draw a picture of your minister?

22 JULY

We should also pray for the men and women who have gone to other countries to tell the people of those countries about the love of Jesus for them. These are our missionaries. They need our special prayers too. They have a job to do for God, but to do it they have had to leave their own country, family and friends. Our missionaries are champions of our faith and need us to support them by praying for them.

Missionaries are the
CHAMP _ _ _ _ of our **FA** _ _ _

23 JULY

Can you fill in the gaps?

- M _ _ T _ N L _ T H _ _ was a hero.
- The verse which Martin Luther loved is found in the book of R _ _ _ _ _ chapter _ verse _ _.
- This verse says:
  The J _ _ _ shall L _ _ _ by FA _ _ _.
- God made O _ _ way for us to get to H _ _ _ _ _ _.
- Heroes DE _ _ _ D their F _ _ H.
- Martin Luther began the REF _ _ _ ATIO _.
- Heroes do what is right even when they are AL _ _ _.
- G _ _ is always with us.
- Heroes need the help of other PE _ _ _ _.

24 JULY

Why don't you choose one of these heroes and write three things you know about them. Tick which hero you pick.

☐ DAVID

☐ DANIEL

☐ MOSES

1 _____

2 _____

3 _____

25 JULY

On the lines below write the words of a prayer you can say for your minister. It doesn't have to be a long prayer. You can copy these words, if you like:-

Dear Lord Jesus,
   please help my minister to be a hero for God.

_____

_____

_____

_____

26 JULY

In this space draw a picture of the hero David and the giant Goliath. Can you find this story in the book of 1 Samuel chapter 17?

27 JULY

If you want to be a HERO for God there are four important things which you need to do.

You must **Hear** what God is telling you to do. You can hear God by reading His words to us in the Bible. God tells us many things in the Bible but unless you read it, you won't know what He is saying to you.

H is for HEAR.

Super Christian

> H is for HEAR we need to
>
> H _ _ _
>
> what God is saying to us

28 JULY

You must **Express** your belief in God. All the heroes we have been reading about talked about God to other people. Unless we are willing to tell others what our beliefs are they will never know our God.

E is for EXPRESS.

> E is for EXPRESS.
>
> We need to tell others about our G _ _

29 JULY

You need to **H**ear what God is saying. You need to **E**xpress your belief in God and you need to be **R**eady to do what is right.

Hero's must be
R _ _ _ _
to do what is right

Our heroes didn't only llisten to God and tell people that they believed in God, they were also ready to do what was right.

R is for READY. We must be ready to do what is right.

Super Christian

30 JULY

H is for Hear.
E is for Express.
R is for Ready.
and **O** is for Obey.

Heroes obey God. We learned what happened to Adam and Eve when they disobeyed God. We learned what happened to Moses when he hit the rock. We learned that when we disobey God, things are changed. Heroes obey God!

Can you find the word hero in this puzzle?

☐ is for hear

☐ is for express

☐ is for ready

☐ is for obey

31 JULY

This month we have been talking about some people in the Bible who were heroes. But we have also seen that heroes are just ordinary people like us. The reason they are heroes, and the reason that we can admire them, is because they were willing to obey God. They wanted to obey God more than they wanted to do anything else. This meant that God was able to help them to be champions!

God will help you to be like these heroes of our faith if you ask Him. Why not ask Him now!

Why not draw a picture of your favorite hero you learnt about this month?

1 AUGUST

A parable is a story that teaches us a moral lesson. That means that it teaches us something about how we should behave. There are many parables in the Bible. The first parable in the Bible is in the Old Testament book of Judges. It is found in chapter 9 of that book and is told in verses 7-20. It is a parable about the trees of the forest that wished to choose from among themselves a king.
This is a lovely story to read.

Can you find the first parable in the Bible.
It is in Judges chapter 9 verses 7-20.

2 AUGUST

When Jesus was on Earth He liked to teach people things by using parables.

Thirty parables which Jesus told are recorded for us in the Bible. These thirty parables can all be read in the books of Matthew, Mark, Luke and John.

How many parables of Jesus are recorded for us?

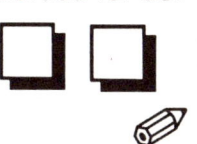

3 AUGUST

The first time we read about Jesus teaching a lesson using a parable is in Matthew chapter 13. Verses 1-23 of this chapter tell us the parable which Jesus used. It is called the parable of the sower.

The last time we read about Jesus teaching a lesson using a parable is in John chapter 10. This parable is called the parable of the good shepherd.

> **The first parable we read about which Jesus told is the parable of the**
>
> S _ _ _ _ .
>
> **The last parable we read about which Jesus told is the parable of the**
>
> G _ _ _ SH _ _ _ _ _ _ .

4 AUGUST

The parable of the sower is a story about a man who went out to sow seeds. Jesus said that as this man scattered his seeds out of their container over the ground, different things happened to the seeds.

• Some of the seeds fell by the roadside and the birds flew down and ate them.

• Some of the seeds fell on to stony ground, which meant there was not enough soil for them to grow proper roots. Without proper roots to hold them firmly in place and to take their food from, these plants withered and died when the sun grew hot.

• Some of the seeds fell among thorns, and the thorns were stronger than they were, so it meant that the young, weak seeds were choked and could not grow.

• But, some fell on to good soil and that meant that they had all the right things to let them grow properly so that they could produce fruit.

> **Four different things happened to the seeds as they were scattered. Can you remember what these four things were?**

5 AUGUST

The lesson which Jesus wanted people to learn from the story about the sower, also had four points to it. He said that when people heard about Heaven they responded in four different ways.

Some people had the truth about Heaven stolen from their hearts by the devil - they were like the seeds that were eaten by the birds.

Some people chose not to keep on believing in Heaven when things in life grew hard, and when other people questioned them about their beliefs. They were like the seeds that had no roots and were on stony ground.

Some people allowed other things to be stronger and more important than the truth about Heaven. They were like the seeds which the thorns choked.

But some people were like the seeds which fell on to the good soil. They heard about Heaven and believed God, and they kept on believing and learning about God, and most importantly, they told others about Heaven.

> **What kind of a person are you?**
> **Which type of seed are you like?**
> **The best type of seed to be like is the seed which fell onto the**
>
> G _ _ _
>
> S _ _ _

6 AUGUST

There are 3 other parables which Jesus told which are about seeds. These 3 other parables are:
1. The parable of the tares.
2. The parable of the seed springing up.
3. The parable of the mustard seed.

One of these is in the book of Mark and two are in the book of Matthew.

Why don't you match the parable to the book and chapter it is found in. First look up the book and chapter and then draw an arrow to the parable that is found in it.

Matthew ch. 13 vs 24-43	Parable of seed springing up
Mark ch. 4 vs 26-29	Parable of mustard seed
Matthew ch.13 vs 31-32	Parable of tares

7 AUGUST

You know the names of four of the thirty parables which Jesus told and which are written for us to learn about.

The four parables which you know about are all stories about seeds. Of course, not all the stories Jesus told were about seeds.

The parable of leaven is a story about yeast. Yeast is the substance which makes bread rise so that it is not flat and hard. This story is a very short story. Not all parables are long stories. Can you find this short parable and see what Jesus taught was like leaven or yeast?

The parable of leaven is found in Matthew chapter 13 and verse 33. In the box you'll find a clue!

Jesus taught leven was like what rhymes with it!

Jesus taught that

H _ _ _ _ _

was like

L _ _ _ _ !

---

8 AUGUST

The parable of the hidden treasure also teaches us about Heaven. Can you imagine how happy you would be if you found a pile of hidden treasure in a field! What would you do? Well, the man in the story Jesus tells about, finds treasure in a certain field and he hides that treasure. Because he is so happy about what he found in the field he sells everything else he has and buys the field! Jesus wants us to be happy about Heaven. He wants us to realise that the treasure of knowing we will be in Heaven is worth more than anything else we have!

Can you find this parable in your Bible?

It is only one verse long.

It is in Matthew chapter 13 and verse 44.

9 AUGUST

The parable about a precious pearl is found in Matthew chapter 13 as well. In fact it is in the second verse after the story about the man who found the hidden treasure.

Find Matthew chapter 13 again and read verses 45 and 46. You will then be able to fill in the gaps in the sentence in the box.

The parable about a precious P _ _ _ _ teaches us that H _ _ _ _ _ is worth more than everything we.

10 AUGUST

Jesus also told a story about a net when He was teaching us about Heaven. This parable is in chapter 13 of Matthew also and is in verses 47 to 50. When you find it you will have found and read four parables which Jesus told about Heaven. They are all in the same chapter of Matthew.

Let's see what can you remember about these four stories?

★ Heaven is like L _ _ _ _ !
★ Heaven is like hidden T R _ _ _ _ _ E.
★ Heaven is like a precious P _ _ _ L.
★ Heaven is like a N _ _.

11 AUGUST

We are going to turn to a different book of the Bible to read another parable which Jesus told. This story is about two debtors. Do you know what a debtor is? A debtor is someone who owes something to someone else. You will find this parable in the book of Luke. Luke is the third book in the New Testament. It is in chapter 7 and starts at verse 41. When you read it fill in the gaps below!

- ★ One debtor owed ☐☐☐ pence.
- ★ One debtor owed ☐☐ pence.
- ★ Both had to pay NO _ _ _ _ _ _ back to the man they had borrowed from.
- ★ The man who owed ☐☐☐ pence was happier about this than the man who owed just ☐☐ pence.
- ★ Jesus said that people whom He forgives M O _ _ , love Him M U _ _ . But people who are forgiven of just a L _ T T _ _ , love Him just a L _ _ _ _ E .

12 AUGUST

Let's go back again to the book of Matthew and find chapter 18. At verse 23 Jesus tells the parable of the unmerciful servant. This story tells us about heaven, about God and about forgiving others. Look at the words in the boxes and see how they remind you of the story.

- The servant who owed the king money
- People who don't forgive others

13 AUGUST

Perhaps the best known parable which Jesus told was the parable of the Samaritan. This parable is found in Luke chapter 10 verses 30-37. There were three people who saw the wounded man in this story. Read it to find out who they were and then fill in the gaps.

★ There was a P _ _ _ _ T

★ There was a L _ V _ _ _

★ There was a S _ M _ _ _ _ _ N

Only one of these people helped the man.

★ The S _ _ _ _ _ _ _ _ _ helped the man.

★ The S _ _ _ _ _ _ _ _ _ also left enough M _ _ _ _ for the sick man to be looked after. Jesus said that we should do likewise when we saw somebody, who needed help.

14 AUGUST

Here is another parable for you to find. It is in the same book as the parable of the Samaritan - that is the book of Luke. This story is in chapter 12 and starts at verse 16. It is a story about a rich fool. When you finish reading it fill in the gaps.

> The rich fool planned to build lots and lots of B _ _ _ _ but he D _ _ _ and never fulfilled all his P _ _ _ _.

Jesus taught us by this story that it is much more important to do the things that are right in life and to love God than it is to worry about planning things that may never happen.

15 AUGUST

Today can you find two parables in your Bible? The first is in Luke chapter 12 verses 35-48. The second is in Luke chapter 13 verses 6-9. This is easy! They are both in the same book. When you have done this, match the Bible book to the parable by drawing an arrow from it to the right parable.

THE RICH FOOL

LUKE 13: 6-9

THE GOOD SAMARITAN

THE SERVANT WHO WAITED

LUKE 12: 35-48

THE BARREN FIG TREE

★ Here is a clue - you have not found these parables yet ★

16 AUGUST

The two parables which you will find today are both stories of things which were lost. They are also both found in the same book and in the same chapter of that book. The book is Luke and the chapter is 15.

Can you find first of all the parable of the lost sheep and then the parable of the lost piece of money.

★ Here is a clue - the first one starts at verse 3 ★

17 AUGUST

Draw a picture of something the prodigal son received from his father when he came home

Like the parable of the Samaritan, the story which Jesus told about the prodigal son is often talked about. Have you ever looked this story up in the Bible and read it for yourself? It is found in the book of Luke and it is in the same chapter of that book as the two stories about the lost things - that is chapter 15. If you already know this story - see if you can find something new about the story that you didn't know before!

18 AUGUST

Do you remember the little bugs called lies which we first learned about when the serpent deceived Eve? The wee bugs that breed and breed and are dirty and ugly and crawl out of our mouths and ears and noses if we don't kill them immediately!

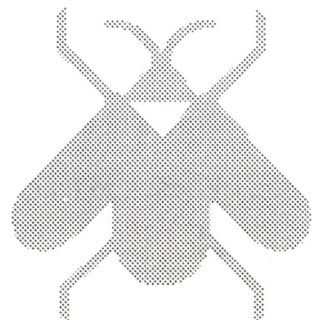

Well Jesus hates lie bugs. Lie bugs have brothers and sisters which are just like them. They are called dishonest bugs.

A man in the parable which you will find today was a man who was dishonest. It is the parable of the dishonest steward. You can read it in Luke chapter 16 verses 1-13.

19 AUGUST

In the same chapter of Luke in which the story of the dishonest steward is found, Jesus tells another parable. Can you find it? It starts at verse 19 of chapter 16.

It is the parable of

the

R _ _ _   M _ _

and the

B _ _ _ _ _

called

LAZ _ _ _ _.

20 AUGUST

Do you know what a judge does? A judge does just what his name says, he decides - he judges who is right and who is wrong and he decides what must be done about it. It is very important that a judge is a just or a fair person. Jesus tells a story about an unjust judge in Luke 18 verses 1-8. When you read this you can fill in the missing words in the box.

The J _ _ _ _ in the parable of the unjust judge was used by Jesus to teach us about the fairness of G _ _.

21 AUGUST

Do you remember who the Pharisees were? They were a bunch of moaners. They moaned about everything! They weren't even happy when Jesus healed people because He did it on the Sabbath. Jesus didn't like the way the Pharisees complained about everybody.

He told a story about a Pharisee and a publican. If you look in Luke chapter 18 again and find verse 9 you can read about the publican and the Pharisee. You will have to read this parable to get the answer for the question in the box!

Who did Jesus say was the man who did what was right?

The PUB _ _ _ _ _

22 AUGUST

In the book of Matthew chapter 20 from verse 1 to verse 16 Jesus tells a story about a man who went out to get people to work in his vineyard. When you read this parable write down how much the workers were paid for their work.

The people who worked were all paid the S _ _ _ .

23 AUGUST

The parable of the pounds is in Luke chapter 19 and it starts at verse 12. Here are three things for you to find in this parable:-

★ Here is a clue - the answers all start with "T" ★

❶ Find out how many pounds the nobleman gave to his servants?   ❶ T _ _

❷ Find out how many servants he gave money to?   ❷ T _ _

❸ Find out how many servants we hear about at the end of the story?   ❸ T _ _ _ _

24 AUGUST

Jesus tells a story about two sons in Matthew 21. These two sons gave two different responses to their father when he asked them to do a job. He wanted them to work in his vineyard. Read verses 28-32 in this chapter of Matthew and find out what the two sons said to their father.

The first son said "I will N _ _ ".

The second son said "I will G _ ".

Now find out what they actually did!

The first son who said he would not go, W _ _ _ .

The second son who said he would go, did N _ _ go.

> Which one of these sons obeyed their Father?
>
> The F _ _ _ _ son.

25 AUGUST

As you will have noticed by now, Jesus told lots of stories about vineyards. This is because the people of the country were Jesus lived when He was on Earth knew what vineyards were like and because many of them worked in vineyards. Vineyards are places where grapes are grown. There is a parable in Matthew chapter 21 in verses 26-46 about a vineyard owner. Can you find this story?

Can you draw a picture of a bunch of grapes?

26 AUGUST

Can you imagine what it would be like if you decided to have a party and invited your friends to come to it and had everything ready... but nobody came!

Jesus in a parable told about a king to whom this happened! This parable is called the parable of the marriage feast.
Find it in Matthew chapter 22. It starts at the very first verse of the chapter. What do you think the king did?
Read the story and see!

27 AUGUST

In Matthew chapter 25 there are two parables.
Can you find them and fill in the names of these stories below?

1. The parable of the T _ _   V _ _ _ _ _ _ _ .
2. The parable of the T _ _ _ _ _ _ _ .

★ Here is a clue • the first story is in verses 1-13 and • the second story is in verses 14-30 ★

28 AUGUST

Sheep and goats are in the parables which Jesus told in Matthew chapter 25. This story is in verses 31-46 of that chapter.
Have you ever read a story about sheep and goats? **Read this one!**

Can you colour in this picture of a goat

29 AUGUST

All the parables which you have found in your Bible so far have been in the books of Matthew, Mark and Luke. Fifteen have been in Matthew. One has been in Mark and thirteen have been in Luke. How many does that make? Can you add them up?

The last of the 30 parables is in the book of John.
It is in John chapter 10.
It is the parable of the Good Shepherd.
It is the most lovely story which Jesus told. Read it and see!

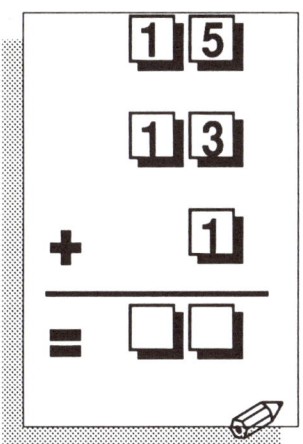

30 AUGUST

In the parable about the Good Shepherd Jesus uses these words:
I am the good shepherd. The good shepherd giveth His life for the sheep.

Can you learn these words. They are found in John chapter 10 verse 11.

"The good shepherd giveth His life for the sheep"

31 AUGUST

You have worked very hard this month and found the 30 parables told by Jesus. You deserve a rest - so instead of reading some more about parables decide which parable you liked best and draw a nice bright colourful picture of it!

My favourite parable

1 SEPTEMBER

In the Bible God has given us ten commandments or rules which He has designed to help us to order our lives. We need order in our lives otherwise everything would be a mess! Now it might seem that ten commandments are an awful lot of rules to learn! But for a start ten isn't a very big number now, is it? You have ten fingers and ten toes - that isn't a huge amount of fingers or toes! This month has 30 days in it. If you learn one commandment every three days you will know the ten commandments by the end of the month because The ten commandments were given first to Moses and you can read them in Exodus - which is the second book of the Bible at chapter 20.

God has given us T _ _ rules to order our lives

$30 \div 3 = 10$

2 SEPTEMBER

The First Commandment says, "Thou shalt have no other gods before me"

Those are eight easy words to understand. The first commandment simply means that we must not put anything or anybody into God's place. What is God's place? God's place is first. He is God. He is the only real God. He should be the most meaningful person in your life because He has made you, given you all that you have and He keeps you and the people you love safe.

Thou shalt have no other gods before me

The first commandment teaches us that God is the only R _ _ _ God and that His place is F _ _ _ _

3 SEPTEMBER

Can you learn the words of the first commandment and then fill in the gaps. Remember you can always look it up in Exodus chapter 20, if you forget!

T _ _ _
shalt have
N _ other
G _ _ _
before M _

4 SEPTEMBER

Can you learn the first part of the second commandment?

Thou shalt not make unto thee any graven image or any likeness of anything, that is in heaven above, or that is in the earth beneath, or that is in the water under the earth

The second commandment is much longer than the first commandment. To make it easy to learn we will divide it into three and you can learn it a little bit at a time. Before you learn the words we will learn the meaning of the second commandment. In this rule God says that because He is the only real God that it is wrong to make ourselves other gods to worship. We should not make statues of things to worship even if those things can be seen by us in the sky or the earth or the sea. No matter how nice they look and no matter how strong they are - they are not God and must not be given God's place.

5 SEPTEMBER

Can you fill in the gaps left in the part of the second commandment which you learned yesterday? If you can remember them try filling the gaps in.

Now that you have filled in the gaps try to learn some more words from the second commandment - It's very long isn't it, but just try reading them.

Thou shalt N _ _ make unto thee any graven image or any likeness of anything that is in H _ _ _ _ _ above, or that is in the E _ _ _ _ beneath, or that is in the W _ _ _ _ under the earth

Thou shalt not bow down thyself to them, nor serve them: for I the Lord thy God am a jealous God, visiting the iniquity of the fathers upon the children unto the third and fourth generation of them that hate me

6 SEPTEMBER

Can you remember the words which you have learned so far of the second commandment? See how many you can fill in:- Can you spot the last words of this commandment? If you learn them you will have learned the **longest** of the ten commandments!

Thou shalt N _ _ make unto thee any graven image or any likeness of any thing that is in H _ _ _ _ _ above, or that is in the earth beneath, or that is in the W _ _ _ _ under the earth. Thou shalt not B _ _ down thyself to them, nor S _ _ _ _ them: for I the Lord thy G _ _ am a jealous God, visiting the iniquity of the Fathers upon the C _ _ _ _ _ _ _ unto the third and fourth generations of them that H _ _ _ me and showing mercy unto thousands of them that love me and keep my commandments

7 SEPTEMBER

You know the first commandment and the second commandment. Maybe you could answer these questions about them!

> **The first commandment says we must not put anything or anybody else in G_ _ ' _ place.**
>
> **The second commandment says we must not make and worship any other person or any other thing except G _ _ .**

8 SEPTEMBER

Now it's time to look at the third commandmandment. Before we learn its words we will look at its meaning. It says we must not use God's name wrongly.

The misuse of God's name makes God very upset. It is wrong to curse using the name of God. God is very strict about this rule and says He will not hold us guiltless if we do this. That means He will hold us guilty for using His name wrongly. We must respect God as a person and we show this respect by treating His name with care.

> **The third commandment says that the misuse of G _ _ ' _ name is W _ _ _ _ and that He will hold us guilty if we do not respect it .**

9 SEPTEMBER

The words of the third commandment are written here. When you learn these words you will now know the first three commandments! To help you to remember the third commandment see if you can put in the missing words:-

Thou shalt not take the name of the Lord thy God in vain; for the Lord will not hold him guiltless that taketh His name in vain

Thou shalt N _ _ take the name of the Lord thy God in V _ _ _ ; for the Lord will not hold him guiltless that taketh His N _ _ _ in vain

10 SEPTEMBER

The fourth commandment is another long one to learn! But don't worry! After you learn this one, the rest are very short! This commandment is about Sunday. God teaches us that Sunday should be a day in which we find pleasure and take a break from the things we do on all the other days of the week. God blesses the Sabbath day - that means He makes it a happy day.

> The fourth commandment teaches us about what we should do on S _ _ _ _ _ .

11 SEPTEMBER

Remember the sabbath day to keep it holy. Six days shalt thou labour and do all thy work: but the seventh day is the sabbath of the Lord thy God: in it thou shalt not do any work thou, nor thy son, nor thy daughter, thy manservant nor thy maidservant nor thy cattle nor thy stranger that is within thy gates; for in six days the Lord made Heaven and earth, the sea and all that in them is; and rested the seventh day wherefore the Lord blessed the sabbath day and hallowed it..

These are the words of the fourth commandment. It will take you a long time to learn these words, so see how quickly you can learn them!

You know God would much rather have you remember to obey commandments instead of saying them and then doing differently!

12 SEPTEMBER

Can you answer these questions on the first four commandments -

★ We must have no other gods except G _ _ Himself.

★ We must not make images to worship instead of G _ _ .

★ We must not use the name of G _ _ as a curse word.

★ We must keep S _ _ _ _ _ a special day of the week.

13 SEPTEMBER

The fifth commandment is about our Mums and Dads. God makes it a rule that we should do as our Mum and Dad tell us. This is because our parents know better than we do, what is right and what is wrong, what things are good for us and what things would hurt us.

Can you use this space to draw a picture of your Mum and Dad?

If your Mum and Dad love God they will never do things that are harmful to you. They love you very much and only want what is best for you. So, God tells us that we should "honour" our parents. If we 'honour' somebody we respect them. If we respect them we do as they ask.

14 SEPTEMBER

The words of the fifth commandment are easy to learn. They are written in the tablet. Read them and then fill in the gaps below.

The fifth commandment teaches us to H _ _ _ _ _ our Father and our Mother. Honour means to R _ _ _ _ _ _ .

Honour thy father and thy mother that thy days may be long upon the land which the Lord thy God giveth thee.

15 SEPTEMBER

The fifth commandment promises us something if we obey our parents. It promises us that our days will be long upon the earth. A promise is something that is definitely given to us. God never breaks His promises to us. He has promised if we honour our parents we will have a long time to enjoy the earth which He has given us.

> **The fifth commandment is a rule with**
>
> **P _ _ _ _ _ _**

16 SEPTEMBER

The sixth commandment says 'Thou shalt not kill'. God does not permit any of us to take the life of another person. God appoints, or decides, when our life concludes on earth. There is no excuse accepted by God if we kill another person. See if you can fill in the gaps in the sentence in the box - It's easy!

Thou shalt not kill

> **God says:**
>
> **Thou shalt not K _ _ _**

17 SEPTEMBER

Thou shalt not commit adultery

The seventh commandment says, "Thou shalt not commit adultery." Adultery is a word that has to do with adults. God tells us that when we are adults when we make a commitment to each other we must not be unfaithful to one another.
This means that when two adults marry they must be true to the person they have married.

The seventh commandment is:

Thou shalt N _ _ commit A _ _ _ _ ERY

18 SEPTEMBER

The eighth commandment is, "Thou shalt not steal." When we think about stealing we usually think about money being stolen or goods being stolen. These are the sort of things which burglars take. But stealing means much more than this.

'Thou shalt not steal' is the

E _ _ _ _ _

commandment

Thou shalt not steal

19 SEPTEMBER

Let's pretend that you have an idea for a new type of super bike! If you told your friend about your idea and showed him your drawings of it, how would you feel if he copied your idea and showed it to someone else saying that it was his idea! You would be mad! - and if you weren't mad, you would be stupid!! Your friend would have stolen your idea!

The eighth commandment, when it says thou shalt not steal - means we must not steal anything, even others ideas!

We must not S _ _ _ _ anything!

20 SEPTEMBER

The ninth commandment is: "Thou shalt not bear false witness against thy neighbour."
Now, what is false witness? Well, false means untrue, and witness means that you have seen or heard something. If you saw two cars crash, you would be a witness of that accident. So, this commandment means that we must not tell untrue things about our neighbours.

Thou shalt not bear false witness against thy neighbour

The ninth commandment says we must not tell U _ _ _ _ _ things about our neighbours.

21 SEPTEMBER

Our neighbours are not just the people who live next door to us! It would be a useless commandment if we weren't to tell untrue things about the people who lived next door, but could tell untrue things about everybody else!! Our neighbours are our fellow human beings. So the ninth commandment means that we must not tell untruths about anyone.

> **Who are our neighbours?**
>
> **Our neighbours are our fellow**
> H_ _ _ N B _ _ _ G _

22 SEPTEMBER

The tenth and last commandment says: "Thou shalt not covet thy neighbour's house, thou shalt not covet thy neighbour's wife, nor his manservant, nor his maidservant, nor his ox, nor his ass, nor anything that is thy neighbour's."
Covet means that we want to own what belongs to someone else!
So the tenth commandment says that it is wrong to long to own the things that belong to other people.

Thou shalt not covet thy neighbour's house, thou shalt not covet thy neighbour's wife, nor his manservant, nor his maidservant, nor his ox, nor his ass, nor anything that is thy neighbour's.

> The tenth commandment teaches us not to C _ _ _ _ .

23 SEPTEMBER

If you break the tenth commandment and covet things that belong to other people you will go on to break the eighth commandment because you will probably steal the things that you covet!
So it is not very sensible to break one commandment, because usually breaking one leads to breaking two, three, four, etc, etc, etc.
The Bible teaches us that if we break one commandment God is just as upset as if we had broken them all.

> If we break just one commandment we upset G _ _ very much.

24 SEPTEMBER

The reason God is upset if we break even just one commandment is because He designed the ten commandments to be of help to us. If you collect a set of something - say a set of trains, and somebody broke one of the models, you would be annoyed. You would still have part of your collection, and it would still be in good condition - but the set would be ruined nonetheless, and its value would not be so great.
The ten commandments are all meant to be kept by us.

> God made the ten commandments to be of H _ _ _ to us. We should keep all _ _ _ of them.

25 SEPTEMBER

How much can you remember about the ten commandments?

★ The first commandment says we must have no other gods, except the real G _ _ .

★ The second commandment says we must not make or B _ _ down to any other G _ _ S.

★ The third says we must R _ _ P _ _ _ God's N _ _ _ and not use it as a C _ _ _ _ word.

★ The fourth says we must make S _ _ _ _ _ a different day from the other S _ _ days of the week.

★ The fifth says we must H _ N _ _ _ our parents.

★ The sixth commandment says we must not K _ _ _ .

★ The seventh says we must not commit ADULT _ _ _ .

★ The eighth commandment says we must not S _ _ _ _ _ .

★ The ninth says we must not tell L _ _ _ about others.

★ The tenth commandment says we must not C _ _ _ _ .

26 SEPTEMBER

Do you remember what happened when Adam and Eve broke the rule which God made about the unique tree? Things changed, didn't they? If we break God's commandments, things will change for us, and we will hurt others by our actions. If we do break God's rules, God will forgive us if we ask Him to. But, if we want God's forgiveness we must really mean that we are sorry. It is no good saying "sorry" and then doing the same bad thing over again! Sorry only means what it says it means if we do not deliberately turn around and be bad again.

God FOR _ _ _ _ _ _ us if we are truly S _ _ _ _ when we do what is wrong.

27 SEPTEMBER

When we obey someone we are showing that person that we trust them. When we trust someone we love them. Jesus said that if we love Him we will keep His commandments. Our obedience of God's commandments is a display of our love for Him and His Son Jesus.

Jesus said that if we love Him we will K _ _ _ His commandments.

28 SEPTEMBER

The ten commandments were given to Moses by God. God talked to Moses and told him the rules which He had made for His people to obey. The place where God talked to Moses was Mount Sinai.

God talked to Moses at Mount S _ _ _ _

29 SEPTEMBER

The rules which God gave to Moses all those years ago are still to be obeyed by us today. These commandments are precious to God and so should be precious to us. If we keep them our lives will be kept in order. We will have a good friendship with God and good friendships with other people.

30 SEPTEMBER

In this space can you draw a big picture of the mountain where God talked to Moses and gave him the ten commandments. Do you remember this mountain's name? If you do fill it in at the top of your picture.

Mount S _ _ _ _

1 OCTOBER

Do you know what contentment is? Well, contentment means that you agree with yourself to be glad.

Now sometimes that's not an easy thing to do! But contentment is one of the greatest things that we can learn to have in life.

In the book of 1 Timothy there is a little verse which says:-
"But Godliness with contentment is great gain"
This verse is in chapter six and it is verse six as well! That's an easy reference to remember, isn't it?

> **Find 1 Timothy 6: 6 in your Bible, learn the words and then fill in the gaps:-**
>
> 'But Godliness with
> **CON _ _ _ _ M _ _ _** is
> great **G _ _ _** .

2 OCTOBER

The first thing in life that we need to agree with ourselves to be glad about is ourselves! Here is a story about a boy who learned to do just that.

Once upon a time there was a wee boy who lived on a unique island. The island had many trees and beautiful beaches. Its grass was long, soft and intensely green. Its sky was blue with grey and white clouds. Sometimes the clouds spilled out tears so that the flowers could grow. Sometimes they sneezed making the trees sway with laughter and sometimes they went away to visit cousin clouds so that the sun could have the whole sky to herself. At night the sky put on a dark velvet blue blanket and instead of cuddling a teddy bear she held a silver-white moon. Around the edge of the island, the sea rolled and splished her waves into scrolls. This was the island of Retsiu.

> **Do you like this island?**
> **Why not try to imagine what it was like.**

3 OCTOBER

Levi lived on **RetSlu**. Levi had purple hair and was seven years of age. Most people are different from others in some way, but Levi thought that his hair made him too different. Actually, Levi had only recently noticed that his hair was purple and it had come as quite a shock to him!
How are you different from your best friend?
Is your hair a different colour? Are you taller or smaller?

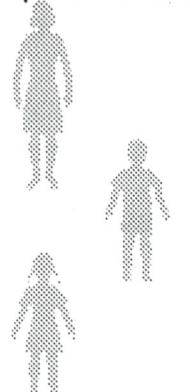

4 OCTOBER

One Thursday Levi's teacher had asked her class to write their weekly essay on "What I hope to be when I grow up". Levi, who hoped to be an artist had written a good answer and the teacher read it to the class. As a result, some of Levi's classmates dedicated him the purple pencil.
Can you colour this pencil purple to match Levi's hair?

5 OCTOBER

At first Levi enjoyed being called the purple pencil and enjoyed the joke but he did wonder why his friends had chosen the colour purple. So he asked his friends - "Why purple?" They laughed! "Because your hair is purple!" So what! thought Levi. Their hair is black and brown and yellow and ginger and black and brown and yellow and ginger… nobody else has purple hair!!

What would you do if you were the only person with purple hair in your class!?

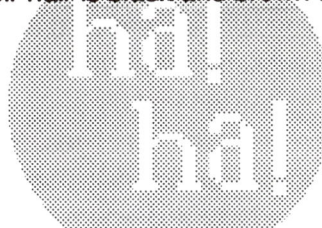

6 OCTOBER

At the end of school that day, Levi listened to all his friends usual teasing remarks.
"Pip, pip, purple pencil!"

"Spasmo's" thought Levi and began his walk home. But all that Levi noticed was people's hair! His teacher had yellow hair. His Mum had black hair like his Dad's. Even Taily his dog did not have purple hair. The paper boy had brown hair and the postman had ginger hair. Have you ever seen a dog with purple hair?!

Can you draw a picture of Taily, Levi's dog?

7 OCTOBER

The days since Levi realised he had purple hair, he spent hiding in his room after school. He only went out for necessities such as to feed Whopper, his pet skunk and Galtic, his locust - or to buy a kali sucker. But today Levi was tired of eating kali suckers and his room felt dull. He also sensed that his pets were becoming restless in their cages. He decided that he would go where no one would ever find him and where he would never be called "purple pencil" again!

Can you draw a picture of Levi's pet skunk in this circle?

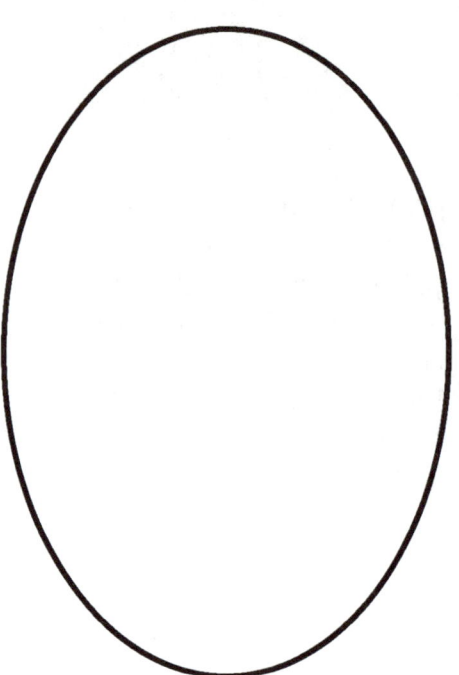

8 OCTOBER

Running into his bedroom, Levi lifted 20 pennies of his savings, his drawing board and jotter, his pencil case and his grey wool cardigan. He collected Whopper, Taily and Galtic and en-route to his hideout he called in the Blue Sweet Shop and bought four kali suckers. Levi arrived at his favourite beach about half an hour later. Soon he found his secret cave. After placing all his belongings in a safe place, followed by his pets, Levi walked out of the cave a little concerned whether or not his actions were extreme!

Do you think Levi was right to go off to his secret cave and hide?

9 OCTOBER

Sitting down, Levi dabbled his toes in the icy salt water and pulled out a kali sucker. Levi looked at the blue of the ocean and thought about being a wave! He wouldn't have to worry about having purple hair if he was a wave! The cool breeze lifted his attention to the rustling trees behind him. If he were a leaf that problem wouldn't exist either - leaves don't have purple hair!! He saw two seagulls argue over a piece of bread and he grew lonely for his brothers!

It's no use, he thought. I will just have to be a hermit artist. I just can't listen to those nicknames all my life.

Do you ever wish you looked different or were somebody else?

10 OCTOBER

As Levi sat thinking about being somebody else or looking differently than he did with his purple hair a robin landed on the rock beside him. "Why are you so sad little artist?" she asked Levi. "How do you know I want to be an artist?" Levi answered. "Well, no one but an artist could possibly have such colourful hair!" replied the robin. "Oh wee robin, do not you see? That is why I am so sad! My hair is purple and I am tired of being nicknamed because of it - so I have left home."

A big smile spread across the little robin's beak.

Can you draw a picture of a little robin with a big smile?

11 OCTOBER

When the little robin stopped smiling she said - "You pathetic little artist, I know how you feel. I too left home because I had red feathers and because people called me 'robin red breast'. When I had flown as far as my wings could carry me, I landed in Africa where I met a giraffe. He became my friend and taught me to laugh when I told him my secret. Do you know what he said to me? He said - Look how long my neck is!! I get teased too. Now, little robin - fly back home and do not be ashamed of your red feathers"

What did the giraffe say that made the little robin laugh?

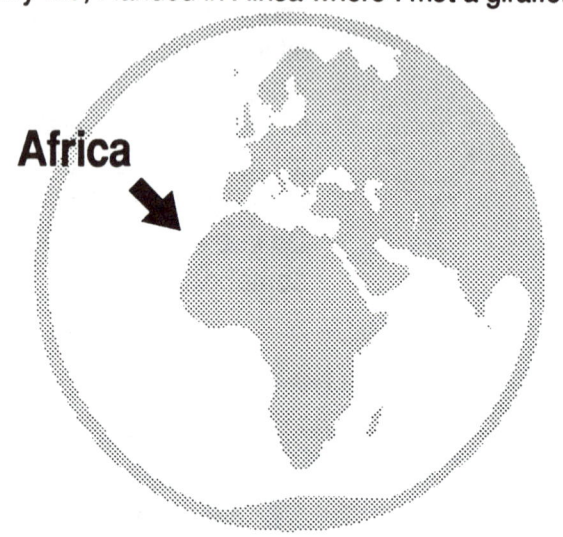

12 OCTOBER

"So," continued the little robin to Levi, "I did just as the giraffe told me and on my way home I began to notice that other animals and people were not all alike either. Now, Levi, go home and paint and you will see that all other people aren't the same!"

"Yes" said Levi "people have different voices, noses, eyes, even their hair is different too! - straight, curly, thick, thin - even none, baldy!!" Levi and the little robin sat and laughed together. "Thank you robin red breast, I will go and paint and enjoy having purple hair." "Good!" chittered the robin as she flew up into the blue sky of Retslu and disappeared behind the trees!

What did Levi now notice about other people?

They were not all the
S _ _ _

13 OCTOBER

Levi finished his kali sucker and skipped back home over the sands to paint, followed by his faithful pets.

Do you know what Levi had learned? He had learned to be content with his purple hair! He had agreed to be glad about the fact that he was different in that way from other people. He learned that everybody else was different too!

What had Levi learned to be?

C _ _ _ _ _ _

14 OCTOBER

When God made us He made us all completely different from each other. Each of us is special to God and God wants us to be glad about ourselves and how He has made us. When we are glad this makes us content.

There is a story in the Bible about a young man who was not content with who he was. This young man was called Jacob.

When God made us He made each of us

D _ _ _ _ _ _ _ _ .

He wants us to be

C _ _ _ _ _ _

with the way He made us.

15 OCTOBER

The story of Jacob is in the book of Genesis. Jacob had a brother called Esau. Esau and Jacob were twins. Esau was his father's favourite and Jacob was his mother's favourite! Esau liked to hunt and Jacob liked to work at home. Esau was the first son and because he was the older twin, he was going to receive what was called his birthright. This meant that as he was by birth the older son he had the right to a special blessing from his father before his father died.

> J _ _ _ _ and E _ _ _ _ were twin brothers.

16 OCTOBER

Because Jacob was his mother's favourite son, she wanted him to have the special blessing. So one day when Esau had gone out to hunt to bring home meat to make a special meal for his father, their mother told Jacob to disguise himself as Esau and to take a meal which she would make into their father. That way Jacob would be given Esau's blessing! This was cheating.

> Who was prepared to cheat to get Esau's blessing?
> J _ _ _ _ _

17 OCTOBER

Esau had hairy arms, so Jacob put some animal fur over his arms to make his arms feel like Esau's. He did this because his father was blind and he knew that his father would feel his arms to see if he were really Esau.
When Jacob went into his father that is exactly what his father did! His father gave Jacob Esau's special blessing.

Can you remember what Jacob did to make him seem like Esau?

18 OCTOBER

When Esau came home his father realised that he had given the blessing to Jacob! Esau was very, very upset and angry. Jacob had cheated him out of his birthright and Esau was so cross he threatened to take Jacob's life. Jacob and Esau's mother heard about this and she got their father to tell Jacob to go to another city until Esau's anger had passed.
Jacob and Esau's parents were called Rebekah and Isaac.

Can you draw a picture of Jacob's arms with the animal fur on them?

161

19 OCTOBER

You can see what happened to this family because Jacob was not content being who he was!
Jacob wanted to be the older twin son, not the younger.
Jacob's mother also was not content with the blessing Jacob would get. She wanted him to get Esau's blessing instead.
When we are not content we are what is called discontent. Discontentment turns us into unkind people who are prepared to cheat to get what we want.

If we are not

content

we are

D _ _ C _ _ _ _ _ T

20 OCTOBER

Because Jacob was discontent he deceived his father and cheated on his twin brother.
If we cheat and deceive we are not making God happy with us - we are in fact making Him very sad.
God wants us to be glad about who we are and what is ours.
He doesn't want us to be discontent with all the blessings He has given to us.

Cheaters and deceivers make God S _ _ .

21 OCTOBER

Do you remember when we were learning the ten commandments, we learned that the tenth commandment is: "Thou shalt not covet".

Jacob was coveting what belonged to Esau. We know that if we covet we long for something that belongs to someone else.

Coveting makes us discontent with what is ours.

> **The tenth commandment says,**
>
> **Thou shalt not C _ _ _ _ .**

22 OCTOBER

Jacob would not have had to run away and hide from his brother if he had been content with being the younger brother and with the blessing that his father had for him. Also - no matter what Jacob did, he could never change the fact that he was the younger twin. So being discontent was a very silly thing for Jacob to be!

> **What could Jacob never change?**
>
> **The fact that he was**
>
> **Y _ _ _ _ _ _**
>
> **than**
>
> **E _ _ _ .**

23 OCTOBER

Can you change the colour of your eyes? Can you make yourself grow taller or grow smaller? Can you change the shape of your nose or the size of your ears? No, of course you can't!

So it is silly to worry about these things isn't it!

God likes us to keep ourselves neat and tidy and He wants us to take an interest in ourselves but He does not want us to become so obsessed with other people that we become discontent with how He has made us.

> **God likes us to be**
> **INT _ _ _ _ _ _D**
> **in ourselves.**

24 OCTOBER

When we are content with ourselves we are free to do things that otherwise we wouldn't have time to do! Contentment makes us free from worry! We are free to improve how we are and enjoy doing that! We can see how much we can learn at school without worrying how much anybody else learns! We can do our favourite things because we enjoy them and not because somebody else does them and we can become our very best in life so that we please God and not worry if we please people like the Pharisees!!

> **Can you draw a picture of what you think a Pharisee looks like?**
>
>

25 OCTOBER

It is important not to worry. If we worry we aren't trusting God. If we worry we are not being content. How can you be glad and worry? You can't!
Besides people who worry - fuss! Fussy people are just like the Pharisees aren't they! Nothing pleases them. Worrying and fussing steal our contentment.

If we worry we are not
T _ _ _ _ _ _ G God.

26 OCTOBER

Do you know why God doesn't like us to fuss and worry? There is no need to fuss and worry.
If your mum had made you a lovely dinner and you were hungry would you eat it and enjoy it or would you go and make another dinner?
You would eat it and enjoy it wouldn't you! You wouldn't go and make another dinner because you wouldn't have to!
God cares for us. He looks after us and He doesn't want us to be fussers and worriers because there is just no need to be like that!

27 OCTOBER

If you had the choice of being happy and content or being sad and discontent which would you choose? Well you have that choice every single day!

Tick yes or no to these questions

	Yes	No
Have you been happy today?	☐	☐
Have you been content today?	☐	☐
Have you been sad today?	☐	☐
Have you been discontent today?	☐	☐

28 OCTOBER

If you are a content person you will help other people to be content and happy too. Contentment shows to our family and friends that we are thankful. God loves thankfulness. Have you said thank you today to God for all He has given you? **Why don't you write down some of the things that you can be thankful for?**

☞ _____

☞ _____

☞ _____

☞ _____

29 OCTOBER

od likes us to thank other people when they do things for us. We should never take for granted the kindness of other people - we should always be sure and thank people for being kind to us. Don't you like it when people thank you?

We should always T _ _ _ _
other people for being K _ _ _
to us

30 OCTOBER

o, you see what contentment is! Contentment brings happiness into our lives, and that means that we can help to make others happy too. That is why the verse you learned at the beginning of this month says that contentment is gain. When we are content we gain gladness. We lose nothing!

Contentment is G _ _ _

31 OCTOBER

Can you remember all the verse about contentment? See if you can fill in the gaps and then write it out yourself underneath.

"But God _ _ _ _ _ _ with c _ _ _ _ _ _ ment is g r _ _ _   g _ _ n."

1 Timothy chapter 6 verse _.

1 NOVEMBER

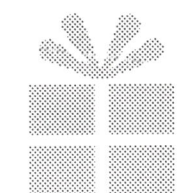

Isn't it lovely to be given a present or a gift! I suppose the times of the year which we most associate with gifts are Christmas time and birthdays.
It is also lovely to give gifts to others isn't it!. It's fun to see them unwrap them and it's fun to see them getting something which they like and want.
The greatest giver of gifts is God.

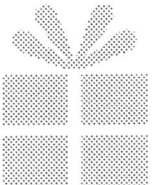

Who is the greatest giver?

G _ _ .

2 NOVEMBER

The greatest gift of all the gifts which God gave to us is the gift of His Son, the Lord Jesus Christ to take the punishment for our sins. Otherwise that big black ✘ would still be between us and God!

What is the greatest gift which God gave us?

His S _ _ , the Lord J _ _ _ _ Christ.

3 NOVEMBER

The reason God gave His Son to the world was His love for us. The gift of love is a gift which we can enjoy each day of our lives. If we were not loved by God and loved by our parents and our families we would not be able to survive. The Bible teaches us that God so loved us He gave us His Son. This is why we love Him.

> **Why did God send His Son to earth?**
>
> **Because He**
> **L _ _ _ _ us.**

4 NOVEMBER

The gift of love is a precious gift which we must be careful with. God wants us to be as generous with our love as He is with His love for us. But, He does not like us to be careless with our gift of love. He does not want us to love unclean things nor wicked things. He wants us to use the gift of love to show our likeness to Him.

> **God wants us to use the gift of**
> **L _ _ _**
>
> **to be like**
> **H _ _ .**

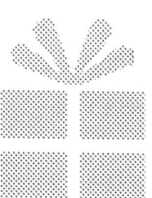

5 NOVEMBER

There are lots of gifts which God has given us. Our health is another gift from God. Nobody can give us health - only God. He created our bodies and makes them work properly. He has given us all the things we need for good health - good food, room to exercise, good water and fresh air. The gift of health is a very important gift.

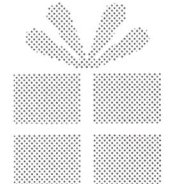

Have you thanked God today for your health?

6 NOVEMBER

God wants us to look after the gift of our health. He wants us to be careful with our bodies as best we can. That is why it is good to not eat too many sweets. That is why it is good to eat fruit and vegetables and food like bread which God has designed to keep our bodies healthy. This is why it is not good to smoke because smoking clogs up our lungs and the nice fresh air which we need to breath to keep healthy can't get into our lungs properly. The gift of our health is something we must look after.

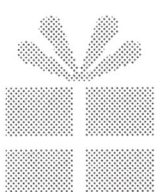

G _ _ wants us to look after our H _ _ _ _ _ _ .

7 NOVEMBER

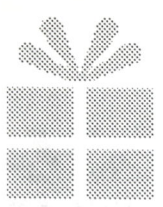

Do you ever wonder where laughter comes from? God made laughter because He likes us to be able to express happiness. Happiness is another gift from God. Imagine what it would be like if somebody told you a joke and you couldn't laugh! Imagine what it would be like if you couldn't smile! God has given us happiness because we are to be a pleasure to Him as our creator.

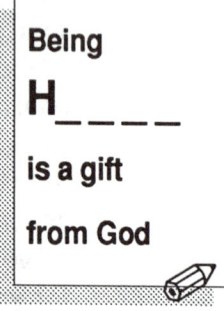

Being

H _ _ _ _

is a gift

from God

8 NOVEMBER

The gift of happiness can be lost if we are disobedient. When we do what is wrong we are not happy, are we? Just like the gift of health, the gift of happiness has to be looked after by us. To keep the gift of our happiness we need to be obedient.

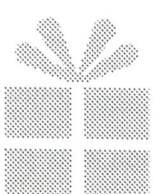

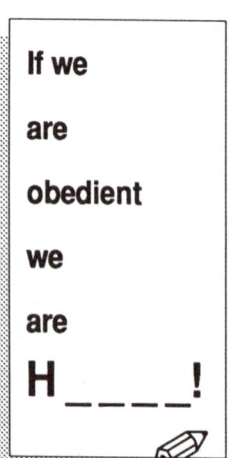

If we

are

obedient

we

are

H _ _ _ _ !

9 NOVEMBER

God also gives different gifts to different people. Some people are very good at mathematics.

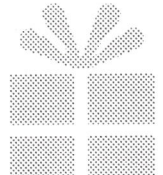

Some people are very good at singing. Some people are very good at painting. Some people are very good at science. The things which we are good at are the things which we call our talents. These talents are gifts from God.

Our T _ _ _ _ _ _ are gifts from God

10 NOVEMBER

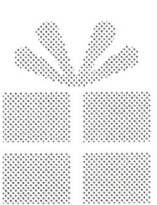

When God gives us a talent it means He wants us to enjoy it and use it. He wants us to learn how to improve it and how to help others with it. God does not want us to let our talents go to waste. He wants us to have full use of our talents.

God wants us to use our T _ _ _ _ _ _ not waste them!

11 NOVEMBER

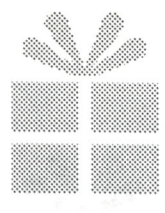

In order to help us to use our talents God has given us the gift of education. That is why we go to school and work. School and work provide us with the opportunity to make use of our talents and to learn more things about our talents.

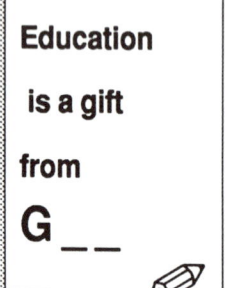

Education is a gift from

G _ _

12 NOVEMBER

God wants us to appreciate the gift of education. Not all boys and girls in the world are able to go to school. Some countries are too poor to provide schools and some people are too sick to go to school. Even though school sometimes is hard work God has given us the chance to learn and to improve our talents.

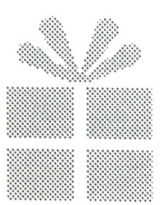

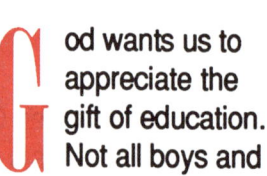

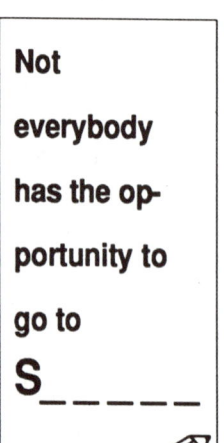

Not everybody has the opportunity to go to

S _ _ _ _ _ _

13 NOVEMBER

Another gift which God gives is the gift of work. After we learn things at school, God provides work for us to do to use what we have learned. God wants us to enjoy our work. We should find pleasure in working. There are many people who do not have jobs. These people are unemployed. It is not pleasant to be unemployed because we need work to keep us happy and to use our talents. People who are unemployed need us to pray that they will soon find work.

The gift of W _ _ _ is a gift from G _ _

14 NOVEMBER

Even though we are still at school we can begin to teach ourselves to take pleasure in work. When you are asked by your Mum or Dad or by your teacher to do a job - you should always be willing to do the job and you should be happy to do the job.
Willingness and happiness make jobs much easier than if we grumble and complain!

Work is easier if we are

W _ _ _ ING

and H _ _ _ _

to do the job.

15 NOVEMBER

God has also given us the gift of our family and our friends. Perhaps you never really thought of your family as a gift - but it is just that. God has given you your parents, your brothers and sisters if you have any, your grandparents and also your friends. He has made them for you and He has made you for them!

God has given us the G _ _ _

of our

F _ _ _ N _ _

and

F _ M _ _ _

16 NOVEMBER

Your family is a special gift. Just as you take care of your favourite birthday present - you should take care how you treat your family. Imagine what life would be like if God hadn't made families! Who would belong to whom! Where would you live and sleep? Who would you love and care for? The family unit is God's way of providing us with a secure home and it is His way of teaching us about love and all His gifts to us. The gift of our family is a very special and precious gift.

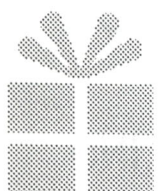

Our

F _ _ _ _ _ _

is a

S _ _ _ _ _ _

gift from

G _ _

17 NOVEMBER

What nationality are you? Your nationality tells what country you are from. Perhaps you are Welsh, maybe you are Scottish, you might be Irish, you might be American, you may be French or German. The country which you are from is another of God's gifts. In your country He has given you many beautiful things. He has made that country especially for its people. Our countries are a gift from God. He created them for us to live in and to enjoy.

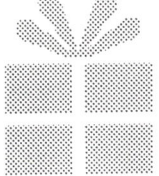

Our country is a G _ _ _ from G _ _

18 NOVEMBER

God expects us to take pride in our country and to look after it. He wants us to care for the things which He has made special to each country. Some countries are good for growing wheat. Some countries are good for raising sheep or cattle. Some countries are good for growing apples or oranges. Some countries are good at producing coal or steel. Whatever our countries have been made to provide - God wants us to maintain that gift and look after it.

God expects us to take care of our

C _ _ _ _ _ _

19 NOVEMBER

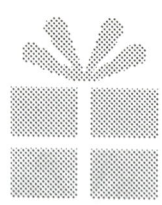

Some of the gifts which God has given to us are gifts which cannot be seen in the same as our country can be seen or our friends and family can be seen. But these gifts are as important. One of these gifts is the gift of God's mercy. God's mercy is God not punishing us the way we deserve to be punished for doing wrong. If we were to be treated by God the way we deserve to be treated, all the gifts which we have been talking about would be withheld from us. But because God is a kind and loving God He has mercy on us and gives us all these gifts!

Can you colour this gift from God and fill in what it is at the bottom?

God's gift of **M** _ _ _ _ _

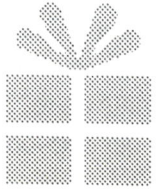

20 NOVEMBER

God also gives to us the gift of justice. Justice is fairness. Not everybody is fair, are they. If you got 10/10 for your home work and somebody else got 10/10 for theirs and they were given a prize and you weren't - that would not be just or fair! God gives us fair and just treatment. He is not unfair. The gift of justice should be copied by us in our dealings with other people.

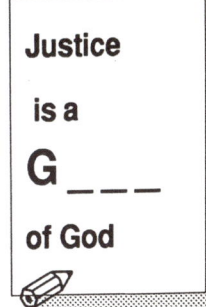

Justice is a G _ _ _ of God

21 NOVEMBER

God's goodness is also a gift. God doesn't have to be good to us - He is God! He could be whatever He wanted to be to us - but He has given good things to us.

Colour this gift

God's gift of G _ _ D _ _ _ S

22 NOVEMBER

God has also given us the gift of truth. He has enabled us to know the truth about our sins and the truth about His Son coming to take our sins away. He has given us the ability to tell truth from lies. Truth is a gift from God.

T _ _ _ _ is a
G _ _ _ from God

23 NOVEMBER

These four things:- mercy, justice, goodness and truth are not just gifts which God has given to us but they are what we call attributes of God. That means they are the very thing which God is himself:-

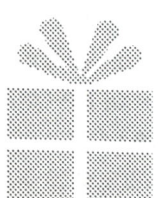

- God is MERCY
- God is JUSTICE
- God is GOODNESS
- God is TRUTH

Can you remember these four gifts? This makes God a Holy God who is sinless and all powerful. This is why God is the only real God.

Our God is the only R _ _ _ God

24 NOVEMBER

Can you fill in the missing gaps?

- God is M _ _ _ _
- God is J _ _ _ _ _ _ _
- God is GOOD _ _ _ _
- God is T _ _ _ _

This makes God a H _ _ _ God

25 NOVEMBER

We learn about the gifts of God by reading our Bibles - so, the Bible itself is another gift from God. We should be thankful for our Bibles because

1. They are written in our own language and because
2. We are free to read them and because
3. They are available for us to own.

Our B _ _ _ _ is a gift from God

26 NOVEMBER

Can you think what it would be like to not have our Bibles in our own language! It would be like going to school and being given all you school books in a foreign language! Some people still do not have copies of the Bible in their own language. Some people are not allowed to read the Bible, it is against the law of their country and some people cannot get a Bible because there are none to buy.

So you can see why our Bibles are a gift, can't you?

> **The gift of having the**
> **B _ _ _ _**
> **in our own language is a very special one**

27 NOVEMBER

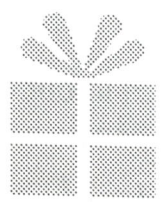

Right at the start of this month we remembered that the greatest gift which God gave to us was the gift of His Son.

This means that the gift of eternal life is ours. Because Jesus died for our sins He made safe for us the way to Heaven so that when our lives on earth are over, we can enjoy the gift of eternal life!

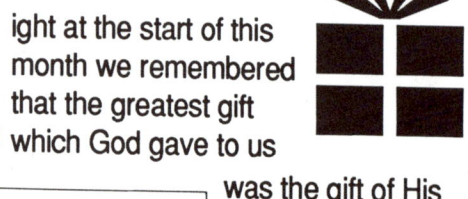

> **The gift of**
> **E _ _ _ _ _ _ _**
> **life is ours because**
> **J _ _ _ _ _ died**
> **for us**

28 NOVEMBER

Why don't you list six gifts which God has given you to enjoy today!

1. _____
2. _____
3. _____
4. _____
5. _____
6. _____

29 NOVEMBER

God teaches us something very special about gifts and giving in the Bible. He teaches us that it is a better thing to give to others than it is to get for yourself! Do you enjoy giving to others? Giving to others makes us like God because God is the greatest giver of gifts. We don't have to go out and buy something to give to others - we can give our love, our prayers, our friendship, our obedience and lots more to others.

What have you given to others today?

30 NOVEMBER

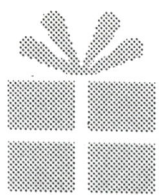

This month we have talked about gifts. Do not forget to say thank you to God each day for all the beautiful gifts He gives you!

Do you think you could copy this verse from the Bible in the square beneath it. I'm sure you could!

> **"The gift of God is eternal life through Jesus Christ our Lord."**
>
> **Romans 6:23**

1 DECEMBER

When God sent Jesus to this earth to die for our sins He sent Him to live among us. In the month of December we especially remember the birth of Jesus. Because Jesus was God's gift to us we give gifts to our friends and family as a reminder of the wonderful gift of Jesus Christ.

In December we especially remember the gift of

J_ _ _ _

2 DECEMBER

Jesus was born on earth and Mary was His mother. Mary was not the mother of God - she was the mother of Jesus, God's Son. Joseph was Jesus' earthly father but God is His Heavenly Father.
Mary was told by an angel that she was going to have a son and that her son would be the Saviour.

Who was Jesus' mother?

M _ _ _

Who was Jesus' earthly father?

J _ _ _ _ _

Who was Jesus the Son of?

G _ _

3 DECEMBER

Even though Jesus was born the way we are born, He was different from us.

Jesus was different from us

he was born of a

V _ _ _ _ _

Jesus was born of a virgin. That means that Mary, His mother, had not conceived Jesus with another human being. God made it possible for Jesus to be born from Mary. We cannot understand how He did this because it was a miracle. But Jesus is God's Son and could not be the Son of any earthly man.

4 DECEMBER

Jesus was sinless. If Jesus had been just like us with an earthly mother and an earthly father, He could not have been sinless. He would have been just like us. The black ✘ of our sin would have been the same on Him as it is on us. But God sent Him to redeem us and to do that He had to be sinless. Jesus, because He was God's own Son was the sinless Lamb of God.

Jesus was

S _ _ _ _ _ _

5 DECEMBER

Jesus, though sinless, still experienced things that we experience. He ate and slept like we do. He was tempted to do wrong the way we are tempted but we give in and do wrong at times - whereas Jesus never gave in to temptation. Jesus, because he was God's Son, could do no sin. If this was not so, Jesus would not have been sinless.

Jesus never gave in to

T _ _ _ _ _ _ _ _ _

6 DECEMBER

If Jesus was not sinless He could not have taken the punishment for our sins. When Jesus was on earth He told us that He was the Son of God and that He had come to do what His Father had sent Him to do - that was to redeem us.
Jesus often used the words "I am" to tell us what He was and what He had come to do.

Jesus often used the words "I _ _ "

to tell us about Himself

7 DECEMBER

Jesus described Himself as the bread of life. He said, "I am the bread of life."

"I am the
B _ _ _ _ of
L _ _ _ "

John _ verse _ _

We need bread to live. Without bread we would starve! Without Jesus we would not have eternal life!
This verse is in John chapter 6 verse 35. Can you find it?

8 DECEMBER

Can you learn this verse and where it is found and write it in this space. Don't peek at the box where you filled in the gaps!

9 DECEMBER

Jesus went on to say that He was the bread of life which came down from Heaven. He said this so that we could understand that God was His Father. He came from Heaven.

Where did Jesus come from?

H _ _ _ _ _

10 DECEMBER

Can you fill in the gaps in this verse and find it in your Bible?

"I am the B _ _ _ _ of L _ _ _ which C _ _ _ down from H _ _ _ _ _."

John _ : _ _

11 DECEMBER

Jesus then said He was the living bread! If something is living it is not dead! If something is living it has energy. Jesus was the living bread. He was better than plain ordinary bread! He had a substance in Him that was greater than the substance of ordinary people like you and me. He is the food that we need for eternal life.

Jesus is the

L _ _ _ _ _

bread

12 DECEMBER

Learn what Jesus said in John 4: 51. "I am the living bread."

Now can you remember the three ways Jesus described Himself that were like bread?

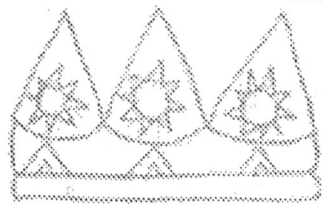

★ "I am the B _ _ _ _ of life."

★ "I am the bread of life which came down from H _ _ _ _ _ _."

★ "I am the L _ _ _ _ bread."

13 DECEMBER

Jesus not only described Himself to be like bread, but He used the idea of light to describe Himself. He said He was the light of the world. Do you remember how important light was in creation? It was the first thing God created because it separated day from night. Jesus is like light. He separates us from our sins. He takes the darkness of our sins away from us.

Jesus is like

L _ _ _ _

14 DECEMBER

Learn what Jesus said:- It's in the box and then when you learn it fill in the gaps in the box below.

"I am the light of the world."
John 8: 12

"I am the
L _ _ _ _
of the
W _ _ _ _ ."

15 DECEMBER

Jesus said that He was one that bore witness of Himself and His Father which sent Him. That means that He could give evidence of who He was. Jesus gave lots of evidence that He was the Son of God to people - He performed miracles - He taught the things of God His Father - He did not sin and He died on the cross.

All these things were the witness or the evidence of who Jesus was.

> Jesus could
> P _ _ _ _
> who He was!

16 DECEMBER

Jesus said, "I am one that bear witness of myself". This simply means that Jesus knew and saw that He was God's Son. He was a witness to it. Just like you can witness who your parents are and know who you are. Jesus was saying I know who I am.

> Can you find this verse in John chapter 8. It is verse 18.

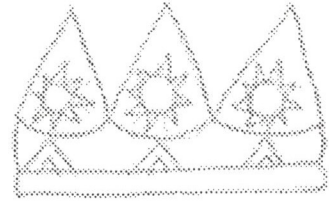

17 DECEMBER

When sheep are being put into their pen to be kept safe they have to use the door into the pen. They can't get in any other way. Jesus said He was the door of the sheep. That means He was the one way into the safety of His Father's home.

Can you draw some sheep safe in their pen?

18 DECEMBER

Jesus also said, "I am the good shepherd". Do you recall the story of the shepherd who went out and looked for the one lost sheep? He was a good shepherd. When Jesus said He was the good shepherd He meant that He came to find us because we were lost from God.

19 DECEMBER

Jesus used sheep twice to describe what He was like - can you remember these two "I am's"?

★ "I am the D _ _ _ of the S _ _ _ _."

★ "I am the G _ _ _ S _ _ _ _ _ _ _."

20 DECEMBER

Jesus secured eternal life for us because He defeated the power of death. On the third day after Jesus was crucified He rose from the dead. When Jesus was explaining this He said "I am the resurrection and the life".

No ordinary, human person could be the resurrection and the life. Only the power of God could defeat death and enable us to have eternal life. Jesus was sent to do this job by God.
Can you find where Jesus said this?
He said it in John chapter 14 verse 6.

21 DECEMBER

Can you fill in the gaps of the verse you found yesterday?

"I am the
R _ _ _ R R _ _ _ _ _ N
and the
L _ _ _ ."

John _ _ : _

22 DECEMBER

Perhaps one of the most famous things Jesus said was "I am the way, the truth and the life". Jesus is the way to Heaven. Jesus is the truth because He is sinless. And Jesus is the life because through Him we have eternal life. These three things are an easy way to remember what Jesus did for us. **This verse is in John chapter 14: 6.**

23 DECEMBER

Let's see how much you can remember about the last two days.

★ "I am the R _ _ _ R R _ _ _ _ _ N and the _ _ F _ ."

★ "I am the W _ _ , the T _ _ _ _ and the L _ _ _ ."

★ Who said these two things about Himself?
J _ _ _ _

24 DECEMBER

Jesus also said He was the true vine. He said this to explain that He was the bearer of good fruit! If a vine does not produce good grapes it is of no use. Jesus produced goodness because He was the Son of God.

Jesus said this in John chapter 15. Can you find the verse?

25 DECEMBER

In the book of John we have found ten "I am's" that Jesus said He was. Can you see how many you can remember?

❶ I am the B _ _ _ _ of life.

❷ I am the B _ _ _ _ of life which came down from H _ _ _ _ _ .

❸ I am the living B _ _ _ _ .

❹ I am the L _ _ _ _ of the world.

❺ I am the O _ _ that bears witness of myself.

❻ I am the D _ _ _ of the sheep.

❼ I am the G _ _ _ S _ _ _ _ _ _ _ .

❽ I am the R _ _ _ RR _ _ _ _ _ N and the L _ _ _ .

❾ I am the W _ _ , the T _ _ _ _ and the L _ _ _ .

❿ I am the true V _ _ _ .

26 DECEMBER

We are the reason that Jesus came into the world! We have been learning that Jesus is sinless, and that He came to do the job His Father sent Him to do - but, there is something else that Jesus is going to do. He is going to return to this earth!

What is Jesus going to do?

R _ _ _ _ _ _ to E _ _ _ _

27 DECEMBER

Yes! Jesus is coming again! Jesus will return to this earth again and those of us who are alive will see Him return! We don't know when He will return just as we don't know when we will die but the Bible tells us that He is coming again.

28 DECEMBER

Are you looking forward to Jesus coming? If Jesus is your friend and Saviour you will be ready and happy to see Him. If you haven't made Jesus your friend by thanking Him for dying for you then you are not ready for His return! **Are you looking forward to seeing Jesus?**

29 DECEMBER

There is nothing to be afraid of about Jesus' return to earth. As a child of God you should be happy and excited about this fact. If you are you will look forward to Jesus' return. If we look forward to Jesus' return we will be ready and prepared to meet Him.

Do you think about Jesus' return to earth?

30 DECEMBER

There is just one day left in this year! God has kept you safe and well all year. Have you thanked Him for doing this? Jesus will soon be coming back - are you looking forward to seeing Him? You know that Jesus is the one way to Heaven, that He lived and died to remove the black ✗ of our sins and that He rose again and lives with His Father in Heaven where He is preparing a place for us.

If you haven't already asked Him to cleanse you from your sins - you should think carefully about doing this right now, because He loves you very much, and longs to be your Saviour and King of your life.

31 DECEMBER

This is the very last day of the year! The words of this song remind us of how much Jesus loves us and how He promises to keep on loving us!

> Wide, wide as the ocean
> High as the Heavens above
> Deep, deep as the deepest Sea
> Is my Saviour's love!
> I though so unworthy
> Still am a child of His care,
> For His word teaches me
> That His love reaches me
> Everywhere!

Happy New Year!

I'd love to hear if you enjoyed this book so why not write to me,
Rhonda Paisley
c/o **Ambassador Productions Ltd.,**
Providence House,
16 Hillview Avenue,
Belfast, BT5 6JR
Northern Ireland